"In a time of Christian leadership thinking and practice that often are not much more than a sacred glazing of a secular ham, Scott Rodin's *Steward Leader* proposition offers a refreshing perspective on the character and volition of those who seek to follow Jesus in their positions of influence. Moving beyond 'how to' formulas, Scott challenges us to examine our 'why to' motivations. His personal transparency, insightful analyses and clarion call to action prepare the way for a revolution in Christian leadership for just such critical times as these."

DAVID J. GYERTSON, Distinguished Professor of Leadership Formation & Renewal, Regent University

"No discussion of leadership is ultimately very meaningful without filtering it through the teachings of Jesus Christ. I have found much that is helpful and inspirational in this book, and I have every confidence that anyone who reads *The Steward Leader* will too."

RICHARD STEARNS, president, World Vision U.S., and author of *The Hole in Our Gospel*

"Scott Rodin's *The Steward Leader* presents a fresh and powerful way to think about what it means to be a Christian leader. In essence, he argues that asking how to become a better leader, or even how to provide more effective leadership, is asking the wrong question. A better question is *How can we be more Christlike as we lead?* Compellingly, Dr. Rodin shows how taming our self-elevating nature and reflecting the image of a triune God revealed in Christ and Scripture will inevitably make us better leaders. He draws honestly upon his vast experience and faithfully upon the riches of Scripture to help us be better Christ-followers. Getting that right will help us be better leaders more than any how-to-lead book ever written (including mine!). *The Steward Leader* is a very valuable guide to any Christian leader who is willing to accept that leading is all about *being*."

BILL ROBINSON, president, Whitworth University

"Finally, a much-needed and long-awaited word on what it really takes to effectively serve the kingdom of our Lord! Rodin, with wisdom and courage, takes the reader on a journey in leading. This text is for serious leaders who are prepared to be faced with the twenty-first-century demand for 'being' over 'doing.' You will be challenged and affirmed by this inspiring, scholarly presentation. This book deserves a place in your library!"

ISRAEL L. GAITHER, national commander, The Salvation Army

"In an age of pragmatism where effective leadership is often defined by outcomes which work, Scott Rodin offers us a refreshing leadership paradigm shift. Rather than focusing primarily on the necessary acquisition of leadership skill sets or leadership development techniques, or the pursuit of outcomes, Rodin maintains that the place for the leader to start and thereafter live is with the unseen part of the leader, the part that God knows and sees."

EUGENE HABECKER, president, Taylor University, and author of
Rediscovering the Soul of Leadership

"The body of work on leadership is so massive that one could wonder if any new words are needed. There are some—and Scott Rodin has offered them in the form of a theology of leadership that is grounded in stewardship and freedom. This book is an inspiring addition to the many writings on leadership theory, practice and characteristics. I believe that those called to lead will find *The Steward Leader* particularly meaningful and formational."

DAVID R. BLACK, president, Eastern University

THE
STEWARD
LEADER

TRANSFORMING PEOPLE,
ORGANIZATIONS AND COMMUNITIES

R. SCOTT RODIN

IVP Academic

An imprint of InterVarsity Press
Downers Grove, Illinois

InterVarsity Press
P.O. Box 1400, Downers Grove, IL 60515-1426
World Wide Web: www.ivpress.com
E-mail: email@ivpress.com

InterVarsity Press® is the book-publishing division of InterVarsity Christian Fellowship/USA®, a movement of
students and faculty active on campus at hundreds of universities, colleges and schools of nursing in the United States
of America, and a member movement of the International Fellowship of Evangelical Students. For information
about local and regional activities, write Public Relations Dept., InterVarsity Christian Fellowship/USA, 6400
Schroeder Rd., P.O. Box 7895, Madison, WI 53707-7895, or visit the IVCF website at <www.intervarsity.org>.

All Scripture quotations, unless otherwise indicated, are taken from the Holy Bible, New International Version®.
NIV®. Copyright ©1973, 1978, 1984 by International Bible Society. Used by permission of Zondervan Publishing
House. All rights reserved.

Design: Cindy Kiple
Images: Paul Tessier/iStockphoto

ISBN 978-0-8308-3878-3

Printed in the United States of America ∞

Library of Congress Cataloging-in-Publication Data

Rodin, R. Scott 1957-
  The steward leader: transforming people, organizations, and
communities / R. Scott Rodin.
    p. cm.
  Includes bibliographical references and index.
  ISBN 978-0-8308-3878-3 (pbk.: alk. paper)
  1. Leadership—Religious aspects—Christianity. 2. Christian
stewardship. I. Title.
  BV4597.53.L43R66 2010
  253—dc22

                                    2009048957

P	20	19	18	17	16	15	14	13	12	11	10	9	8	7	6	5	4	3	2	1
Y	27	26	25	24	23	22	21	20	19	18	17	16	15	14	13	12	11	10			

CONTENTS

INTRODUCTION

This is not a "how" book on leadership, but a "who" book. It is more about heart than hands, more about transformation than transaction. It does not start with the traits of successful leadership, but with the intent of our Creator and the journey of transformation to which we are called. It is not about what God wants us to do as leaders, but about who God is, and what that means for our self-understanding and our vocation as image bearers of God who are called to lead.

This book is an invitation to a journey. The journey begins with seeking to understand the heart and nature of the God we seek to serve and in whose image we have been created. The journey continues by seeking to answer the question of who we are as godly stewards responding to the heart and nature of God. The journey brings us into the place where we can begin to answer for ourselves the question of our identity and purpose in life.

This is a journey of transformation from owners to stewards, from kingdom building to submission, from bondage to freedom and from obligation to joyful obedience. It begins with our personal transformation as godly stewards. And it continues when we are called to lead.

My prayer is that this approach will present readers with a fresh set of lenses for considering the call to leadership in God's kingdom. Rather than being driven by the traits of leadership, this journey will take us from a biblical, holistic understanding of our calling to be godly stewards first, and move us to an understanding of what it means when godly stewards are called to lead.

The call to be steward leaders is based on fundamental convictions.

Part two will lay the foundation for these convictions and then move us to an understanding of the four-part character of the godly steward. As we live in relationship to God, self, neighbor and creation, we respond to God's grace through our journey as his faithful stewards on all four levels at which we have been created and redeemed.

Again, we are first called to be godly stewards and then to be leaders. Commitment to our call as stewards guides us as steward leaders. But we are stewards first. It is as stewards who undergo the daily transformation of the Holy Spirit that we are sometimes called to lead.

Take note that this is not a discussion about steward*ship* or even leader*ship*, which direct our attention to principles or skills someone might use to lead. Rather, this book's focus is on the transformed steward of God, who is also called to be a leader. It is about the "who," not the "what" or the "how."

I will conclude by offering ideas about how the life of the steward leader affects the people he or she serves, and through them the organizations the leader is called to lead. I call these "trajectories." They are not methodologies, steps, processes or programs; the work of the effective steward leader resists such boxes and boundaries. These four trajectories illustrate a dynamic, Spirit-led process that is able to adapt itself to whatever situation the steward leader may be called upon to lead. Therefore I can only attempt to point in the direction such work might take, and I leave it to you to fill the blanks with the endless possibilities that are a part of your vocational calling.

This reconsideration of leadership serves, in the end, as an invitation and, consequently, calls for a response. So, here at the beginning, I will ask you the questions with which I will end this study:

- Are you prepared to go deeper in your faith than you have ever gone before?

- Are you ready to be used by God in more powerful ways than you thought possible?

- Do you desire to bless the people you serve and the organizations you are called to lead?

- Are you ready for the journey?

Everywhere we go, God is at work. This is his redeemed world, and we are his redeemed people in this redeemed world. As such, we are all on this journey together. We are all moving from the old to the new, the broken to the restored, the lost to the found. It is a process based not on our action but on the work that has been completed for us in Jesus Christ. Therefore, our calling is one of participation in his work, already inaugurated and commenced.

Steward leaders are willing and active participants in the great work that God is doing in the world. The effectiveness of their leadership is solely dependent on the great work that God is doing in them, transforming their hearts and minds to be like his. This, again, is a willing and active participation in the work of Christ begun before the foundations of the world. How awesome is that!

This book is about the "who" of the steward leader as a reflection of the "who" of God. It is a journey that ultimately sets us free because it calls us closer to the one who came to set us free. It is a journey that calls us to an abundant life of active participation through joyful obedience, because it is centered on the one who came that we may have life, and have it abundantly. It results in fruitful and meaningful ministry and organizational effectiveness. And it produces in us and through us praise, confidence, peace and joy—those fruits that reflect the image of our abundant and gracious God.

Our triune God stands ready to equip and bless every godly steward who is called to lead. He offers us the gifts we need and the power to resist the temptations we face. What awaits us is *freedom* and the call to a life of *joyous obedience*.

Do you want that for yourself, your marriage, your people and your ministry? If so, welcome to the journey!

PART ONE

BECOMING A STEWARD LEADER OF NO REPUTATION

THE JOURNEY OF THE STEWARD LEADER BEGINS at an intensely personal level. For that reason I want to begin by sharing some personal reflections on my own journey and on what I have learned along the way.[1] This includes a confession.

Over my nearly thirty years in not-for-profit management and consulting, I have held a number of leadership positions, including development department head, seminary president, association president and company president. I have also held important leadership positions such as father, husband and church member.

Here is the confession: in my roles as a leader I have been mostly wrong. Now, I was not wrong about everything. In fact, I believe I have been right about a lot of things I have attempted and accomplished in these roles. I could create the usual list of "legacy" items that we leaders make in justifying our time in leading others. There is much I am thankful for, many moments to treasure and certainly a legacy that I trust will make a difference to generations that follow.

Yet at the very heart of my reflection on my various roles lies the major conclusion: I was wrong in my understanding of leadership in Christian ministry. I was also wrong in my expectations of others and myself. And, what may be the hardest to admit, I was wrong in my motives.

I look back and wonder how I went so wrong. I was brought up in a relatively functional home with wonderful parents and a good relationship with my siblings. My career path had certainly prepared me for leadership: years of fundraising experience, a Ph.D. from a leading school in Great Britain, successful work in not-for-profit administration and a knack for strategic planning and vision casting. I had good experience in managing effective teams and working with not-for-profit boards. There was no lack of preparation for the task.

Nor was there a lack of motivation. I had long believed that God had gifted me for leadership. I rose naturally and quickly into key leadership positions wherever I went. It felt right, seemed natural and was usually satisfying and challenging. So it was natural for me to take leadership roles as they came along.

My problem was not with preparation, motivation or even with a lack of a sense of calling or sincere desire to serve God with the best of my skills and abilities. The problem lay solely with my understanding of the nature of Christian leadership.

At any moment in my trajectory as a leader, if you had asked me for a Scripture that epitomized the leadership ideal, I likely would have pointed you to Nathan's directive to King David, "Whatever you have in mind, go ahead and do it, for the LORD is with you" (2 Samuel 7:3). I could identify with David as "God's man at God's time," and I believed that God would pour out his wisdom and favor if I could be such a man. After all, there were kingdoms to conquer and people to be led. There were great things to be done for the Lord, and no vision was too limited, no goal too small.

Reflecting back on my leadership experiences and the leadership I have witnessed in my years of consulting, I would now point to a different verse. In speaking of Jesus' incarnation, Paul tells us that Jesus "made himself of no reputation, and took upon him the form of a servant" (Philippians 2:7 KJV). It does not say that Jesus became a man of *bad* reputation or of *questionable* reputation, but simply of *no* reputation. That is, reputation, image, prestige, prominence, power and other trappings of leadership were not only devalued, they were purposefully dismissed. Jesus *became* such a man, not by default or accident, but by intention and design. It was only in this form that he could serve, love, give, teach and, yes, lead.

In reflecting on my years in the seminary president's office, the church and the living room, I have come to the conviction that true Christian leadership is an ongoing, disciplined practice of becoming a person of no reputation and, thus, becoming more like Christ. In his reflections on Christian leadership, Henri Nouwen refers to this way as resisting the temptation to be relevant. "I am deeply convinced," he wrote, "that the Christian leader of the future is called to be completely irrelevant and to stand in this world with nothing to offer but his or her own vulnerable self."[2] In the past I rejected this idea outright. Today I see and affirm this way of no reputation as the heart of godly leadership.

My journey from the one verse to the other marks a significant progression for me. The former verse was a direct word spoken from God to a specific person, and I extrapolated it to apply to me and to Christian leadership in general. The latter verse was a description of the nature of Jesus, whom I am called to follow—simply and humbly. The former focused on God's blessing on my work, the latter on my response of obedience and submission to his nature.

This study of the steward leader has grown out of a combination of my work in holistic stewardship, my study of leadership and these honest reflections on my journey. Taken together, I am learning that everything flows from the transformed heart of a godly steward. As godly stewards we do indeed offer only our vulnerable self, but we can do so with confidence and great joy. That is a very different journey from the one I began two decades ago.

In the following five areas, I've begun to learn what it is to be this sort of steward leader. In each area I have had to confess my misunderstanding of Christian leadership. I've also had to embark on a new journey of transformation that leads to freedom and the joyous obedience of a steward leader.

Anointed Versus Appointed

I know of few Christian leaders today who were anointed before they were appointed. We have mostly employed the business model of doing careful searches, looking for Christian leaders whom we can appoint to office. We check their credentials, put them through rigorous interviews and give them psychological tests before we make the critical appointment. Once they are in place, we then anoint them and ask God to bless their work.

The biblical evidence seems to indicate that God selects leaders in the opposite order. Samuel anointed David before appointing him king. The selection criterion for leadership was not based on who seemed most fit for the appointment, but on whom God had anointed for the task. And appointment without anointment always led to disaster.

I have never been asked in a job interview if I sensed God's anointing for a position. If I had, I don't know how I would have answered; the question never entered my mind.

Anointing is critical to the task of Christian leadership because of its nature as a unique form of leadership. Christian leadership, which I define as the work of the steward leader, requires nothing less than a complete, wholesale submission of your life in service to God and God only. It is the "losing of your life" to the work that God wills to work in you to benefit your institution, school, church or organization.

And the stakes are high. Nowhere else in the Christian life is the price of divided loyalties so costly for so many for so long. Ineffective and fallen leaders compromise kingdom work, and the effects are both temporal and eternal. Therefore, leadership must be entered with the utmost seriousness and only when you have clearly been anointed for the task. I have no criterion to offer or search process to recommend in determining anointing, but I am convinced that this biblical model needs to be taken more seriously during the selection of leaders.

With God's anointing comes what every leader seeks: God's power and presence. A special blessing is bestowed on God's anointed. It is the blessing of his power manifest in ways only seen through the work of his chosen. God's anointed shout, and walls fall. They lift their feeble staff, and seas part. They speak God's Word boldly, and movements are begun that free the souls of the oppressed. God's anointed do the miraculous because they are servants of the Almighty. Without this anointing, we are continually thrown back on ourselves to make things work. With it, we have the resources of heaven at our disposal if we will be faithful servants.

Anointed leaders do anything God asks. Anything. They seek God's will with a passion. They do not move without anointing, and they are not diverted from their course once they have it. God's anointed love what God loves and hate what God hates. That means loving God's people, God's church, God's environment, God's resources and God's plan. It also means hating sin in every form and coming against anything that stands between God's loving plan and its accomplishment. God's anointed are people of keen discernment. They are branches solidly engrafted into the true vine. God's anointed are servants first, last and always. And they have only one passion: to know and do God's will that he might have the glory. In this way, God's anointed are people of no reputation.

I did not come into leadership positions with a clear sense of anointing as a leader, but I now better understand and value the distinction between appointment and anointment. I believe that God's anointing can rest on steward leaders who submit everything to him. God works through leaders who trust him beyond question and rely on him for the totality of their life and work. Anointing begets submission, and submission is the disposition of the heart of the steward leader.

Fighting the Need to Increase

When John the Baptist saw Jesus walking in his presence, he made the declaration, "He must increase, but I must decrease" (John 3:30). Most Christian leaders would say they wish that Jesus would increase and they would decrease. But it is hard to decrease in a leadership position. Natural trappings distinguish those in leadership, such as salary, title, prestige, priority, power, influence, honor and advancement. And in each area lie tempting opportunities for increase. There are also motivations to build a kingdom in which we house our growing collection of leadership trappings. Not only must we meet this desire for the fame and fortune of leadership with resistance, but, according to U.S. President John Adams, we must also have "a habitual contempt of them."[3] Nouwen is even more direct:

The way of the Christian leader is not the way of upward mobility in which our world has invested so much, but the way of downward mobility ending on the cross. . . . Here we touch the most important quality of Christian leadership in the future. It is not a leadership of power and control, but a leadership of powerlessness and humility in which the suffering servant of God, Jesus Christ, is made manifest.[4]

Perhaps the hardest place to decrease is in the influence and the power we hold over people and decisions. For this reason we find Christian leaders who are overly directive at best and autocratic at worst. As a result we produce churches and ministries that are rife with learned helplessness. By overestimating our worth we help our people depend on us for everything. And that dependence feeds into our need to be needed, to be the visionary, to be in control. We tell ourselves that the more we lead in this way, the more our leadership is valued and our presence desired.

Of course, this is not real leadership but a counterfeit that contributes to *our* increase and expands *our* kingdom. This type of leader is an owner-leader. This leadership does a terrible disservice to people, leaving them uninvolved and underdeveloped. It wastes resources and limits ministry, all under the guise of strong leadership and the use of God-given talents for "getting things done." Leadership pioneer Robert Greenleaf reminds us that the difference between a true servant-leader who is servant first and a leader-servant who seeks leadership first lies in the growth of the people who serve under him or her. The test question is, "Do those served grow as persons; do they, *while being served*, become healthier, wiser, freer, more autonomous, more likely themselves to become servants?"[5]

Steward leaders are stewards over the people they serve. They cultivate people. Leadership bent on self-centered increase lacks integrity and is usually dishonest. Integrity bears witness externally to all that we are internally. It does not derive from or depend on what is external, on an external increase. For that reason, godly integrity begins with our inner life in God.

Stephen Covey sees integrity as "the value we place on ourselves."[6] He means that we first must keep faith with ourselves if we are to be trusted and trustworthy to those around us. We must keep the promises we make to our own value system. We will see that for steward leaders self-confidence must be founded on faith in Christ and a desire to be like him—in fact to be indwelt by him—in every way. We must seek to be Christlike in our inner being and be confident that "he who began a good work in you will carry it on to completion" (Philippians 1:6). If Christ is truly living in us, as Paul reminds us, we can in turn live for others with integrity in our work.

As steward leaders we have no need to seek to increase in our positions of power. We have no desire to build our own kingdoms and advance our own reputations. Our lives are "hidden with Christ in God" (Colossians 3:3), and therefore it is no longer we who live, but Christ who lives in us (see Galatians 2:20). It is only with this kind of godly integrity that we can seek to decrease as we look away from ourselves to see Christ increase in and through our work as leaders.

Steward leaders empower their people, give away authority, value and involve others, seek the best in and from their people, and constantly lift others up, push others into the limelight and reward those they lead—all so that God's will may be done in a more powerful way. They seek no glory for themselves, but find great joy in seeing others prosper. They take no account of their reputation, but desire that Jesus' face be seen in all they do. Leadership expert Max De Pree's definition is worth repeating: "The first responsibility of the leader is to define reality. The last is to say thank you. In between the leader is a servant."[7]

I have come to understand that the call of the steward leader is a call to a lifestyle of an *ever-decreasing* thirst for authority, power and influence, where our quest for reputation is replaced by confidence in the power of God's anointing.

Being and Doing

I am a doer. I have the reputation of going one-hundred-plus miles per hour, always focused on accomplishing objectives, meeting deadlines and crossing things off my formidable to-do lists. I like results over process, action over deliberation, the tangible over the theoretical. And I like to lead people to accomplish goals and realize vision. What gets in my way are processes, people with "issues," using time inefficiently and undertaking work that seems irrelevant. I say I am committed to transformation, but it must get done on schedule and show some real results.

The problem with this style of leadership is that is denies the truth of the gospel and our creation in the image of God. If we are truly made in the *imago Dei*, our perception of God will necessarily and significantly influence our self-understanding. If we view God as a solitary monad, an isolated being known for power and transcendence, we will be leaders who reflect those characteristics. We will be lone rangers, seeking power and focusing on doing. We will see people as means to an end and value the product over the process. If we see God as a distant and detached monarch, we will lead as monarchs.

If, however, we are true to our trinitarian historical commitments, we learn that relationship is what defines us. We learn that to be God's people we must focus on who we are as people in relationship. We learn that leadership must be concerned with the whole person and that God's intent is for us to *do* the work of the kingdom within and through the community of believers. This is the journey of transformation from which we develop the heart of the steward leader.

A proper understanding of our creation in the *imago Dei* also teaches us that what is most important to God is not what we do but *who we are*. Secular leadership experts are waking to the fact that the key to leadership effectiveness is self-awareness.[8] In Christian terms this means that the leader, through self-awareness and self-criticism, is the one who is transformed first.

Greenleaf recalls the story of a king who asked Confucius what to do about the large number of thieves in his country. Confucius replied, "If you, sir, were not covetous, although you should reward them to do it, they would not steal." Greenleaf goes on to say,

> This advice places an enormous burden on those who are favored by the rules, and it established how old is the notion that the servant views any problem in the world as *in here*, inside himself, and not *out there*. And if a flaw in the world is to be remedied, to the servant the process of change starts *in here*, in the servant, and not *out there*.[9]

Before God can do a great work in an organization, that work must be done first in the heart of the leader. Unless God has taken our hearts captive, all of our good "doing" lacks spiritual integrity and Christlike authority. Our work exposes the absence of God's anointing. At the exact moment we think we have it all together, we cease to be usable in the work of the kingdom.

If I could put one Bible verse on the desk of every pastor and every Christian leader in the world, it would be this: "If we claim to be without sin, we deceive ourselves and the truth is not in us" (1 John 1:8). As steward leaders we must be engaged in a constant process of self-evaluation and repentance. It is so easy for us to be tempted in a variety of directions, and when we stray, we affect our entire ministry. Steward leaders undertake their work with deep humility and a keen awareness of their weaknesses and shortcomings. They know themselves well, seek accountability, pray fervently and watch carefully for red flags and warning signals.

Nouwen challenges us to seek this defining characteristic of Christian leadership.

> The central question [of the heart of Christian leadership] is, are the leaders of the future truly men and women of God, people with an ardent desire to dwell in God's presence, to listen to God's voice, to look at God's beauty, to touch God's incarnate Word, and to taste fully God's infinite goodness?[10]

For this reason the greatest tool for effective steward leaders is a mirror and a group of friends to be sure they are looking into it with clarity and focus.

Becoming a leader of no reputation means not being afraid to stare down your weaknesses and uncover the messy stuff in your private world. It means letting God transform you. And more importantly, it means knowing how much you need that transformation, far more than anyone else in your organization. When this ongoing transformation is added to the desire to decrease while Christ increases, all under the anointing power of the Spirit, the steward leader begins to emerge.

Leadership Is a Miracle

One of the greatest gifts I received during my term as seminary president came from my colleague Ron Sider in the form of a book titled *Leadership Prayers* by Richard Kriegbaum. The honesty and humility in the prayers bear witness to the heart of a godly leader. In his prayer for trust Kriegbaum offers these words:

> I love you, God. You know I do. How natural it is to love you. You are perfect. You are beautiful, pure, powerful, absolutely truthful, and kind. You have been so generous to me that just saying thank you seems pitiful sometimes. But far more powerful in my life is knowing and feeling that you love me. You know exactly and completely who I am—all my ugly thoughts, my mangled motivations, my pretending, my irrational fears, my pride, and my unfaithfulness—and you still love me. *I know you love me. You know me, and yet, because you love me, you let me lead others. I do not understand it, but I am grateful.*[11]

As I read these words back through the lens of my experience, I come to the conclusion that when God uses any of us to lead effectively, it is nothing short of a miracle. When we place the complex and demanding role of a godly leader next to an honest self-awareness of our sinfulness and incompetence, we are thrown wholly on the grace of God and his faithfulness if we are ever to lead anyone anywhere.

This miracle is analogous to what occurs both in the efficacy of Scripture and in the effectiveness of our preaching. In both, human words are taken up by the power of the Holy Spirit to become the words of God. In both its inspiration and its interpretation, the words of Scripture rely completely on the activity of the Spirit of God. When the Spirit illumines the human word, hearts are changed, people are transformed, and God's work is done. The same is true in our preaching. We study and prepare as we are trained to, but in the end our preaching becomes effective only when the Spirit of God takes up our feeble human words and uses them to touch hearts and change lives. When it happens, it is a miracle!

Conversely, when the written words of Scripture or the spoken words of the preacher stand alone, apart from the work of the Spirit, our ministry loses its power. It becomes *our* words, *our* interpretation, *our* exegesis and *our* proclamation. And slowly and naturally into these words of ours seeps the ugly thoughts, mangled motivations, pretending, irrational fears, pride and unfaithfulness noted in Kriegbaum's prayer.

We must approach leadership in the same dependent humility. The sole responsibility of the steward leader is joyous, responsive obedience. Throughout history God looked to the least, the weakest, the outcast, the untalented, the sinful and the rejected to give great leadership at historic times. I don't think he has changed that approach today. If we are honest as leaders, we know that our capacity to lead is easily exceeded by the size and complexity of our call. We know that there are others more talented, more prepared, more spiritual and more courageous than are we. But great, godly leaders have always worked at that miraculous intersection where humility and faith meet the awesome presence and power of God's Spirit—and the miracle of leadership happens.

It doesn't mean we don't prepare ourselves, hone our skills and seek to be the best we can be for the kingdom. What it does mean is that, in the end, all that we bring will fall woefully short of what is required, and we will be ever thrown again into the grace and faithfulness of God to work the miracle of leadership in and through—and even in spite of—our small pile of skills and talents.

When God uses us to lead effectively, we should fall on our knees in wonder and thanksgiving that we have seen again this miracle worked in our midst. However, it is far too easy for us to take ownership of the miracle and to believe that the results are due to our own wonderful abilities and innate leadership qualities. If and when we make this subtle yet devastating shift, we become owner-leaders, and the efficacy of our leadership for the kingdom is over. We are on our own, cut off from the power and preservation of the Spirit. Most every leader will find him- or herself at that place at some point in his or her work, and it is a terrifying place to be.

Godly leadership is the miracle of God's use of our earthen vessels for the glorious work of his kingdom. To miss this miraculous aspect of leadership threatens everything we do as leaders, and our office or study will become the loneliest place on earth. I have come to better appreciate the miracle of godly leadership and its connection with self-awareness, the need to decrease and the power of God's anointing as a defining characteristic of the steward leader.

Seeking the Right Applause

One of my bookmarks carries a thought that has stayed with me throughout my years in leadership: "It doesn't matter if the world knows, or sees or understands, the only applause we are meant to seek is that of nail-scarred hands." Leaders are exposed to opportunities to generate applause. It can come in the form of commendation from the board, approval of our decisions by employees, recognition of our institution's work by constituencies, admiration of our leadership abilities by coworkers, and words of appreciation from family and friends.

As public figures we receive both undue criticism for the failures of our institutions and unmerited praise for their successes. The true calling of leadership requires us to accept the former and deflect the latter. That is, our job is to take the blame for mistakes made by those under our leadership and to deflect the praise by redirecting it to those most responsible for our success. In this way we keep ourselves in balance, never taking the criticism too personally and not accepting the praise too easily. But this balance is very difficult to maintain.

Yet keeping this balance leads to the relatively unusual experience of finding freedom in leadership—a central concern of this book. Steward leaders are *free*! We can know freedom from the tyranny of self-preservation and advancement only as we accept criticism and deflect praise. The success of the steward leader lies significantly in his or her ability to keep this twofold movement of leadership in balance. Leaders who inflict pain lose trust and dishearten their people. Leaders who absorb praise produce resentment and sacrifice motivation.

Two significant temptations come into play here. The first is the fear of rejection that causes us to run from confrontation. It comes when we desire to make everyone happy and to measure our performance, our effectiveness and our "leadership" by others' approval. We are motivated by the idea that good leaders will not generate conflict and that rejection of our performance as leaders is a rejection of our personhood and character.

The second temptation is to lead by reacting. We see which way the wind is blowing and steer that direction, regardless of the situation. We do not want our people to be anxious, to question our decisions or to disagree with our reasoning. We want harmony and unity, which is commendable. But left unchecked, this desire causes us to sacrifice courage, vision and risk taking. It brings us momentary applause, but ruins us in the end. To paraphrase a quote from Ralph Waldo Emerson, "Some leaders worry themselves into nameless graves, while here and there some forget themselves into immortality."

So we must ask ourselves just what kind of applause we are seeking. If human applause serves to validate, affirm and encourage us, we also find that it binds us, boxes us in and ultimately strangles us. When our daily self-worth and the measure of our effectiveness come primarily from the reaction of those with whom we work, we are finished as leaders.

Consider how many decisions you are called on to make in any given day—some in private, some in meetings and some in the public arena. Every day come multiple opportunities to make applause-generating decisions. Sometimes the temptations to make them are enormous, especially when considering the price to be paid if other alternatives are chosen.

Now consider how often God's will and following his Word point you down a different path. This path is the journey of the steward leader. True leadership takes place at the intersection of doing what God is telling us to do and doing the expedient and popular thing. It is there that we know to whom we are looking for our affirmation.

The goal of the steward leader must be to go to bed every night with a clear conscience and a right heart before God. God asks only one thing of steward leaders: that we seek with all our hearts to know his will and respond obediently and joyfully.

Before taking on one of my leadership positions, I spent a couple of hours with a man whom I respect for his wisdom and leadership abilities. He gave me encouragement and good advice, and before I left, he told me something that both inspires and haunts me to this day: "Scott, in whatever you do, always strive to be a man that God can trust." I now believe that the man or woman God can trust is the one who seeks only the applause of nail-scarred hands. For that person, the cultivation of reputation carries no value.

Leadership Is Transformation

My years in various leadership positions are a study in transformation. I came into so many of them with a wrong set of expectations, values and ideas about Christian leadership. I was not thirsty for power or obsessed with the trappings of leadership, but I also was not seeking to be a leader of no reputation, nor was I responding to the call to be a servant *first*.

And it was here that I was wrong.

I used to reject the notion that good Christian leaders were only those who were brought kicking and screaming into the position, and that anyone who wanted to be a president or CEO or superintendent or executive director should be automatically disqualified. I still reject some aspects of this as not entirely in keeping with our giftedness and our desires. However, the truth in this view is that steward leaders are godly stewards first, and it is as godly stewards that they are called to lead.

For those who see themselves as leaders first, the temptations to stray in leadership are enormous. As Nouwen wrote,

> The long painful history of the Church is the history of people ever and again tempted to choose power over love, control over the cross, being a leader over being led. Those who resisted this temptation to the end and thereby give us hope are the true saints.[12]

I arrived at this point in my own steward's journey with a dramatically transformed understanding of the godly leader, an understanding that continues to be transformed today. In the end, our work as steward leaders is all about lordship. Before it is about vision casting or risk taking or motivating others or building teams or communicating or strategic planning or public speaking, it is about lordship. When Jesus is singularly and absolutely Lord of our life, we seek to be like him and him only. That is our sole calling. We are called to our work, and that work carries God's anointing. We are called to decrease that Christ may increase. We are called to *be* the people of God before and as we *do* the work of God. And we are called to pray and look for the miracle of leadership that God may work in our midst.

In these ways, in responding faithfully to this calling and striving after these ideals at the cost of everything else that may tempt us, we become steward leaders. And as we do, we will be transformed into the likeness of Christ, becoming leaders of no reputation.

PART TWO

THREE FOUNDATIONS

1

LEADING IN THE IMAGE OF THE TRIUNE GOD

"Let us make man in our own image, in our likeness,
and let them rule over the fish of the sea, and the birds of the air,
over the livestock, over all the earth and over the creatures that move
along the ground." So God created man in his own image, in the
image of God he created them, male and female he created them.

GENESIS 1:26-27

He is the image of the invisible God, the firstborn over all creation.

COLOSSIANS 1:15

Do not lie to each other, since you have taken off your old
self with its practices and put on the new self, which is being
renewed in knowledge in the image of its Creator.

COLOSSIANS 3:9-10

I was raised in the church and spent my entire life in it. I was baptized as an infant in the Lutheran Church–Missouri Synod. As a faithful young Lutheran I attended confirmation classes when I turned twelve and prepared to go before the board of deacons to affirm my faith and proclaim my understanding of the basic tenets of the Christian doctrine according to Luther's Small Catechism. I did well.

Later I became a youth director, went on to graduate biblical studies after my college years and prepared for doctoral work in theology. Along the way I served my church as an elder, taught Bible study classes and preached on occasion.

Despite all this time in the church, in formal study and in Scripture, it wasn't until one day in a doctoral-level seminar that I embraced the radical idea (radical to me, at least) that I had been created in the image of a *triune* God. Now, you can think me pretty dense, but over the years I have tested this idea with a good number of devout, intelligent and well-read Christian brothers and sisters, and the response has been the same. Most everyone said that they "always kind of understood that," but few had ever stopped to consider its transformational implications.

If you are willing to consider this concept and its implications for your life and work, join me in thinking theologically for a few moments. I want to define stewardship by going back and thinking about God's intention for his beloved creation.

We begin with a central tenet of the Christian faith: *you and I were created in the image of the God we know in Jesus Christ, who has revealed himself to us as the triune God of grace.* That may be the most profound statement human ears have ever heard. The implications are enormous, pervasive and unequivocal.

Here is the fruit of this amazing truth: when we know with certainty the nature of our Creator God and the image that we bear as his children, we can know with equal certainty the purpose for our existence. This certainty leads us to a life that has meaning as we live out that purpose, bearing God's image in community. It is an invitation to a new kind of life, to contentment, to real joy and to freedom. Let me unpack this truth in a little more detail.

God's self-revelation to us in Jesus Christ is the core of our faith, giving it direction and substance. It is in God's self-revelation to us in Jesus Christ that we can know the heart of our God, and know it with *certainty*. The good news of the gospel of Jesus Christ is that we have been invited into a relationship that assures us of the knowledge of God that is sufficient for a life of meaning, purpose, freedom and joy. Jesus Christ came to us to reveal the heart of God, the character of God, the Word of God and the will of God for us (see Colossians 1:15-20; John 12:25-26; 14:6-7; 17:6-10).

What a marvelous and incredible truth: we know the heart, the character, the words and will of God, and we know them with certainty. While this knowledge is provisional, fragmented and always "but a poor reflection" (1 Corinthians 13:12), it is nonetheless sufficient.[1] That is, we are not left groping in the dark for some additional knowledge of God that is crucial for our lives but remains unavailable to us.

This is a critical and foundational position for us, given the scriptural affirmation that we have been created in the image of God. We are created to reflect God's image in our world through what we say and do. Imagine how absurd it would be to try to reflect the image of a God who chose never to reveal himself, herself or itself to us in any reliable (certain) way. God would be a deceiver if he called us to reflect his image as our primary purpose in life but remained so hidden that we were constantly thrown back on ourselves to figure out what that image really looks like.

We lived in Scotland for four years while I completed my Ph.D., and we attended our little community "kirk." Sunday services were simple and somewhat "dreak" (somewhere between dreary and bleak); often the highlight was a children's sermon given by one of the parishioners. One Sunday the clerk of session, a gray-haired gentleman with barrel chest and booming voice, came forward to give the talk. The children ran up front to gather around him, including my three children, then ages three to seven. He told them a story from his youth, when he and his best friend would sneak into a neighbor's garden and steal strawberries.

I recall his retelling of the story: "One day when we went in to steal strawberries, the owner climbed up and hid on the wall of the garden behind a tree, where we could nay see him. As we were filling our pockets with berries, suddenly he jumped down off the wall and grabbed us, and took us off to our parents' houses, where we received a right good beating." And then, with all the children glued to his every word, he leaned over, looked them straight in the eye and concluded, "Children, that's how God is. So you better be good lads and lassies."

I was horrified, and I all but ran my kids home after the service, put them on the couch and told them, "That is *not* how God is!" I imagined what life must have been like for our clerk of session, who spent his entire life thinking that God was hiding up on a wall somewhere, waiting to catch him out. What an image to bear!

It is only by knowing God in Jesus Christ that we can embrace our call to reflect the image of God. It is a clear and joyous, albeit difficult, calling. The three Scriptures at the beginning of the chapter show a progression. We were created originally in God's image (Genesis 1:26-27), Christ came bearing and restoring that image (Colossians 1:15), and we are now being transformed as bearers of that image (Colossians 3:9-10).

Building on that certainty, we can take the next step in affirming that the God whose image we are called to reflect is *triune*. It is Jesus who reveals to us the triune nature of God *in himself*. In Jesus we come to know that the Father sends the Son in the power of the Spirit. Jesus points us to the Father and empowers us in the Spirit. And Jesus sends us out to "make disciples of all nations, baptizing them in the name of the Father and of the Son and of the Holy Spirit" (Matthew 28:19).

The implication for us is that we were created and have been redeemed to bear the image of a God who is in his very nature community, fellowship and interdependence. God did not reveal himself as a single, solitary, distant monad up there somewhere in the universe. Our God is a God *in relationship*. That is not just his choice; it is the very content of his being.

We cannot respond to this God by bearing an image that is individualistic (reflecting a singular, monarchical God), singularly self-reliant (reflecting a detached, deistic God) or distrusting and cynical (reflecting an absent and capricious God). Our knowledge of the nature of our triune God gives certainty not only to his nature, but also to our own nature, calling and purpose.

Reflect on these two fundamental questions of the Christian faith before we move on: First, do you really believe that you can (and do) know the heart and nature of your Creator with sufficiency and certainty in and through Jesus Christ? A steward must know the heart and will of the Master. There is no reason to live another moment in uncertainty. Our Creator is a God who loves us, is for us and created us to live in relationship with him. We know this in Jesus Christ, and therefore we know it with certainty.

Second, if you know this certainty for yourself, does your life reflect the image of a God who is, in his very nature, relationship, fellowship and community? Have you bought into the individualism of much of our culture, or do you witness to a calling that enmeshes your life with those around you? A steward must represent the heart of the Master.

My prayer at this early moment in our journey together is that your spirit is at peace in the knowledge of the heart of your Creator and that your life is a testimony to the triune nature of a God in relationship, who was revealed to us in Jesus Christ.

The Image of God: Created, Lost and Restored

If we are to understand our call to be steward leaders, we must start with a definition of the godly steward. Everything I will develop will flow from this definition:

> As God's people, we are called to reflect the image of our Creator God through whole, redeemed relationships at four levels—with God, with our self, with our neighbor and with creation—bringing glory to God and practicing in each the ongoing work of the faithful steward.

This definition follows the central story of Scripture from creation to Fall to redemption and its promise of final restoration. Our call to be image bearers of the triune God must be understood in all three parts of the story and at all four levels of our created nature. Simply put, our fourfold nature was created in perfection, lost in sin and restored in Christ. Our understanding of our vocation as steward leaders emerges from this fourfold nature and three-part story. Let me walk with you through the beauty of this wonderful story as it relates to our call as leaders in God's kingdom.

The image created—meaning and purpose. We were created to have meaning and purpose in our existence as image bearers of God. In the first three chapters of Genesis, we find that we were created for whole relationships that reflect the image of God on four levels: our relationship with God, with our self, with our neighbor and with creation.

As Adam and Eve lived out those four levels of relationship, they reflected the image of God. And so do we. The meaning of our lives is to be image bearers of our triune God in all four of these relationships.

1. Relationship with God. On the first level our life has meaning when we are at peace with our Creator. Augustine stated it clearly in the opening page of his *Confessions*: "Thou awakest us to delight in Thy praise; for Thou madest us for Thyself, and our heart is restless, until it repose in Thee."[2] The reality of our created nature is that we are shaped and formed for the distinct purpose of living in relationship with our Creator God. Without such a relationship we are set afloat to spend our lives searching for ways to find meaning. When called to lead we are plagued by a restless spirit. We are easily knocked off balance if we try to lead others when we are not at peace with our Creator and do not have an internal sense of life's meaning in Christ. Wandering, unsettled leaders cannot provide certainty and meaning to the people they lead.

The first couple knew this peace and intimacy in the absence of sin. Today, it is in the redemptive work of Jesus Christ that we are restored and reconciled again to God. We cannot do it for ourselves. This relationship has been bought for us with the highest possible price, the blood of Christ. God's original intent in creation is now the gift given to us to steward with gratitude and praise.

If we were created for intimate relationship *with God,* then our purpose is to love God with all our heart, soul, strength and mind. This is our first and highest calling and joy. Worship, sabbath rest, devotion, prayer, fasting, study, praise and presence are ways in which we fulfill our purpose in our relationship to God. Intimacy is not something we create; it is the result of total surrender that allows God to do something in us and for us. God draws us near as we submit ourselves to him. And our first and highest response is praise. *Purpose at this first level is measured in intimacy and doxology.*

2. Relationship with our self. Meaning on the second level—our relationship with our self—is found in a self-understanding and an acceptance of ourselves that is balanced and honest in the light of our true relationship with our triune Creator and redeemer God. This balance keeps us from being pulled into self-satisfaction on the one hand and self-deprecation on the other. Honesty plants our feet on the solid knowledge that we are prone to rebel through our sinful nature, yet also empowered to live holy lives through the regenerating power of the Holy Spirit. Leaders who are at peace with themselves can lead others with humility and grace. Leaders who find meaning in both their weaknesses and the wonder of God's work within them can provide balance, honesty and integrity to the organizations they serve. The first couple needed only the presence of God and the certainty of their place and calling in relationship to him to know that peace.

If we were created for relationship *with our self,* our purpose is to have absolute certainty of who we are, why we are here and what we are to do. This self-understanding was a part of God's loving intent for us when he created humanity in his image. His purpose for us is found in the balance in our self-perception between the beloved child of God and the sinner saved by grace. It is humility *and* courage; it is the simplicity of the clay vessel *and* the complexity of being the workmanship of God. It is the amazingly powerful place between our recognition that apart from Christ we can do nothing and our recognition that in Christ we can do all things. *Purpose at this level is measured by balance in our self-image and the extent of our reliance on God as the sole caretaker of our reputation.*

3. Relationship with our neighbor. Meaning on the third level—our relationship with our neighbor—comes from an investment in the lives of others as a response to our nature as relational beings and the outworking of our relationship to God through Christ and in the Spirit. As God is triune in his very nature, so we were created to find meaning in our existence in community. Leaders who find meaning in their relationships to others engender in people a sense of individual worth and communal connectedness. When relationships are valued, communities, teams and families are endowed with meaning that reflects our created state before our triune God. The first couple lived in fellowship and community with one another as the natural expression of being image bearers of the triune God.

If we were created for relationship *with our neighbor,* our purpose is to love our neighbor as we love ourselves. We were created to see our neighbors and their well-being in the same way we see our own, which calls us to value relationships as ends, not as means to be used for our own benefit. *Purpose at this level is measured by the needs of our neighbor, and not our own needs. It is the extent to which we build and value relationships as God's gift and as ends in themselves.*

4. Relationship with creation. On the fourth level—our relationships to the created world—meaning is derived from our status as caretakers of the created world. From Genesis we see that we were created primarily for this activity. The first task given to God's image-bearing creatures was to tend the garden (see Genesis 1:28-30). When we reflect God's caring nurture of us by caring for and nurturing his creation, we find meaning in a world that screams at us that meaning is found only in the hoarding and consumption of resources. Scripture demonstrates for us that we were created to find meaning in the sharing and careful stewardship of God's abundance. Leaders who love the creation that God loves and who value the stewarding of all of God's resources can lead people to the same ends.

If we were created for a relationship *with creation*, our purpose is to live in harmony with creation; to love it, to tend it, to take care of it. God's command is that we have dominion, rule over and subdue the earth just as God has dominion, rules over and subdues us. *Purpose at this fourth level is measured by how loosely we hold to our possessions and how closely we heed our call to be caretakers of creation.*

Our identity as children of the triune God lies in our lives lived in and through community in holistic relationship, mutually interdependent and seeking the unity of the Spirit. That is how we reflect the image of a triune God. This life glorifies God because that is precisely why we were created. That is our purpose. We fulfill this purpose when we live as we were created to live—in whole, healthy and productive relationships that reflect the image of God on all four levels. In each we find the purpose of our lives as God's new creation.

The image lost—brokenness and deceit. We know that when sin entered the world, it had a devastating impact on our relationship with God. However, too often we have thought the effects of the Fall apply only to our relationship with God. Here we must be sure to continue our commitment to think theologically and holistically as we consider the effects of the Fall on all four levels.

In the fall of Adam and Eve into sin, our *relationship with God* was fatally disrupted. Sin caused separation from God that could be overcome only by the blood of Christ. The God known in intimacy and fellowship in Eden became the holy and terrible God who was approachable only through ritual sacrifice, human mediation and a constant need for a repentant heart that seeks unmerited forgiveness. Far from walking with God in the cool of the evening, the first couple now found only fear and trembling in God's presence. To look upon God was sure death. To even say the name of Yahweh was blasphemy. He is often characterized between Eden and Bethlehem as consuming fire, rushing wind, thunder, earthquake and blinding light. The once-intimate relationship between Creator and creature was all but destroyed, being held together only by the unending grace of the God of the covenant.

We also experienced the loss of *relationship with our self.* Adam and Eve lost their primary purpose in life—tending the garden, loving one another and fellowshipping freely with God as his beloved creation. We can see how, since the Fall, the central theme of the history of humanity became our search to get back what was lost, to find God again and be at peace with creation and our Creator. We are all on a search to recapture intimacy with God and certainty of purpose and meaning in life.

The impact of this loss cannot be overstated. When we lose this guiding sense of purpose, we are untethered from our moorings and float through life seeking for some other place where we can find security and refuge. Yet every other port disappoints. Every place we look for validation of our own self-worth ultimately fails us, whether our occupation, friends, family, wealth, fame or even religion. We also can use our position of leadership as a grasping for this meaning. Regardless of the means, each one will feed back to us a distorted and conflicted image, leaving us once again afloat on a sea of relativity when we so desperately seek a sense of certainty. It is a despairing place to be.

This self-deception renders every act of sin as ultimately a sin against our self. To sin is to perpetuate the lie that we are still slaves to sin, that evil still holds sway over us, that we have not been "bought with a price," that we are still under the penalty of sin and death. When we sin, we attempt to undo—and thereby deny—the person we truly are in Christ. We become a stranger to our self. This is the root of the problem of the loss of our self in our sinfulness and fall. Yet it is all we have outside a trusting and grateful relationship with our Creator.

To understand the root of this loss we must return for a moment to the first couple standing naked and unashamed in the garden. In this pre-Fall moment there was no possibility of self-definition that did not include being in right relationship with others. To know oneself was to know oneself in true relation to God, to the other and to creation. There was no act in which the self was considered abstractly apart from others. To be human meant to be male and female together. It meant to be creatures of God in fellowship with God. It meant to be a caretaker and partaker of creation. Humanity had no basis for being apart from these relationships. Therefore the "self" was confident, at peace and whole as it participated in what gave it its definition, meaning, purpose and function.

To be human was to be a steward, for the work of stewardship was the natural result of these relationships. The self-understanding of the first couple was expressed not only by who they were but also by what they did. They were stewards in relation to all around them. Their command was to be fruitful, multiply and replenish the earth. Their command was to have dominion and care for the earth just as God had already modeled dominion and care for them and all creation. Being stewards and following these commands were part of their self-understanding. In our original created state, being and doing were enmeshed.

The Fall cost the first couple this sense of self-identity. They lost it when they were forced to consider themselves in abstraction from their relationships. Instead of asking, "Who am I in relation to God?" they were left to ask, "Who am I over and against God?" In other words,

"Who am I alone?" Who is man without woman, woman without man, and woman and man over and against creation? If we can no longer define ourselves by our relationships because of their brokenness, we must define ourselves according to some other criteria—an inevitably foreign and counterfeit criteria. The rise of the autonomous self and the search for independent self-understanding and meaning has forged a different standard for self-definition, and therefore an alternate set of criteria to measure meaning and purpose.

- What are the standards you use to measure your success?
- How are these standards affected by how you are seen by your neighbor, your spouse, your kids, your boss?
- We all establish certain measures of our self-value and our ultimate worth. What are yours?

It should not be surprising that these criteria are rife with the deception that has come with our fallenness at every relational level. They come wrapped in terms of power, dominance, personal happiness, self-actualization and self-gratification. They have become the prize that many will sell their souls to gain. They are the end used to justify almost any means, even if hurtful, exploitative, devious or perverse. In dismissing our original purpose—God's criteria—we must replace it with another.

Despite all of this, we must never lose sight of the fact that we never ceased to be God's beloved creation. God's covenant with us, where he would be our God and we would be his people, was established for us before creation and in full knowledge of the work of Jesus Christ, which would restore to us what was lost in the Fall.[3] Our loss of self-definition does not nullify the fact that we are still the beloved creatures of God. That ultimate self-definition will never be lost as long as God is the God of the covenant.

Our struggle is with sin's ability to keep us from recognizing our true original and abiding reality. We struggle to see in ourselves what God sees in us in Christ Jesus. Our worth, which is great in the eyes of God, is marked by broken relationships at every level, feeding back to us the accusation of our utter worthlessness. This is the state we find ourselves in as a result of the loss of our self-definition in the sin of Eden.

The other side of this problem is the choice we make to replace that loss of self-definition with alien definitions. The enemy will always be more than glad to offer sumptuous substitutes for our self-definition as children in the kingdom of the triune God of grace. It began in Eden with "I am an individual man," and "I am an individual woman." These new definitions were twisted substitutes for "I am man with woman," and "I am woman with man." We have a seemingly limitless array of self-definitions. Whether they are formed from natural traits, behaviors, social circumstances, achievements or patterns of reinforcement from others, they always stand on very shaky ground. In every case, if they are in denial or defiance of God's definition of us, they are innately deceptive and can work only for our destruction.

Whatever attributes currently make up our self-perception, our work as steward leaders depends on submission of those attributes to the redemptive and transformative authority and lordship of the great definition given to us in the covenant established for us by the triune God before the creation of the world and brought to fulfillment for us in Jesus Christ, the Son of God incarnate. We are first God's children— children in the kingdom of the triune God of grace.

All other self-perceptions must come under that all-encompassing reality. To do this we must become stewards of our self-perceptions. We must be caretakers of our self-definition so that we do not allow alien perceptions to distort our self-understanding as children of God. We can do that only by the working of the Holy Spirit and in full knowledge of what was done for us in the work of Jesus Christ.

With sin also came the rise of *enmity with our neighbor.* Adam blamed Eve; Eve blamed the serpent. The very next story that comes after the Fall is Cain's killing of Abel. Thus begins the human history of "man's inhumanity to man." This inhumanity is a product of the dethroning of God and the coronation of the self as the primary driving force in our life. This replacement of God with self is the core definition of the impact of sin in our life and its subsequently devastating affects on our relationships with one another.

Perhaps the single greatest indicator of this loss is the tendency we have to use our relationships with our neighbors as means to serve ourselves. Take networking as one example. For many, the core value in networking is the use of relationships to further an agenda. The very term speaks of working *through* people to get where you want to go. I subscribe to Linkedin, Plaxo, Facebook and other online networking services, and I must watch to be sure that my purpose is to build redemptive relationships and not solely to be in the network to further my own agenda and meet my own needs.

Like all tools, the Internet can be used redemptively to build relationships for kingdom purposes and connect people like never before. But even when we seek to use it as a resource for the kingdom, we must acknowledge the ever-present temptation to use our networks solely to meet our own needs and goals: more business, better jobs, new opportunities, season tickets and so on. The Internet has provided the lowest relational requirement for the expected return of any medium in human history. Relationships as means are the norm. Relationships can become stepping stones, avenues and pipelines that take us to where we desire to go and help us secure the things we think we want and need. And all at seemingly so little cost to us. Since Eden we have been on a quest to use our neighbor to further our own good, and now we have the perfect tool to accomplish it.

In the rise of the individual and autonomous self the Fall brought about another movement within the creature. The effect of the Fall was to refocus the creature's attention away from serving the Lord and toward a counterfeit form of lordship. By grasping at the chance to be like God, the creature changed from being the "servant of the Lord" to being the "Lord over servants." Theologian Karl Barth said, "Wanting to act the Lord in relation to God, man will desire and grasp at lordship over other men, and on the same presupposition, other men will meet him with the same desiring and grasping."[4]

We have changed from seeking servanthood to seeking power, from being life-givers (a beautiful definition of the steward) to life-takers,[5] from finding meaning in relationships to finding meaning in a position that places one over and against another in relationships. In the Fall the simple command to love our neighbor as we love ourselves has become an impossible task, in part because we have lost our ability to love ourselves as God loves us, and in part because we have lost the intimacy with the God who is the author of that very love. A loss of relationship with God brings about a distorted self-image, which in turn leads to abusive relationships that serve a self that is still desperately searching for its source of meaning and purpose.

Finally, in this original sin, we see the rise of conflict in our *relationship with creation*. It is after the Fall that "dominion" was redefined as *domination*, "rule over" became *own and control*, and "subdue" became the justification to *exploit*. It is a post-Fall understanding of these words that has yielded the grossly mistaken assumption that the earth is ours to use any way we want. The result has been the hoarding of resources for our own use and the ravaging of creation to exploit those resources.

This is the inevitable final step in a process that began with the loss of our relationship with our Creator. With the loss of that all-defining center, the self rises up and takes control. It is a distorted self that seeks meaning in those things that are *self*-serving. That includes how we relate to people around us and to the created world in which we live. This self-serving nature distorts our view of our world. It places us in an alien relationship to God's creation. Outside of Eden we are at once at enmity with creation, and we respond by assuming the role of its lord and master. We play the absolute owner of that which is God's alone. In our role as lord, we use this creation to serve our own purposes. No longer identified as God's gift to us, creation becomes a commodity that we can use to meet our needs, which, apart from a relationship with our Creator, are never satisfied.

This is the final scene in this devastating picture of humanity after the Fall. Brokenness with God leads to a distorted self-image. This marred image gives rise to the self as the center of life, which in turn uses people and creation in its futile quest for meaning and satisfaction. It is a desperate state, but God did not leave us here.

The image restored—the rise of the godly steward. Praise be to God that the restoration Christ accomplished through his blood was even more holistic than the affect of the Fall. Paul tells us that, although one transgression brought sin into the world, *how much more* the blood of Christ covers all sin (see Romans 5:9-15). He also proclaims, "As in Adam all die, so in Christ all will be made alive" (1 Corinthians 15:22). And we are assured that, while sin brought condemnation on the one man, so the blood of Christ brings redemption for all humanity (see Romans 5:12-15). In short, *all* that was lost in the Fall was *fully and completely* restored in Christ! Just as sin brought brokenness on all four levels, so Christ's redemption brought healing and reconciliation on all four levels.

In Jesus' life we have demonstrated the right relationship we seek with God, our self, our neighbor and our world. Jesus lived the life we could not live. He was obedient where we were disobedient; he was faithful where we were faithless; he was a neighbor when we passed by on the other side. He knew who he was, why he was here, what his ministry was to accomplish. He knew his place before God, in the world and among his people. He did all this while bearing our humanity! He completed in his life and confirmed in his death and resurrection the full requirements of the original relationship between God and his creature. By doing so Jesus Christ redeemed our relationships at all four levels.

A holistic understanding of Christ's atoning work assures us that our *relationship with God* was reestablished. Through the life, death and resurrection of Christ, we have been reconciled to God. The book of Hebrews rejoices that in this newly restored relationship with God in Jesus Christ we now "approach the throne of grace with confidence" (Hebrews 4:16).

There is an important place for our response in this overwhelming grace. Our response to grace does not undermine the fact that our relationship to God has been fully restored in Christ. But the freedom of response does mean that, while we cannot undo what God has done, we can deny it, reject it and live in rebellion against it. We can act as children of the devil, we can side with evil, we can scorn our mediator, but we cannot undo the cross or resew the torn curtain of the Holy of Holies.

The blood of Christ has atoned for all humanity, and therefore God's relationship to us is forever changed. We can choose against that grace, we can choose for hell and our own destruction, but that does not change the work of God for us in Christ. Our choice affects how we will respond to God's grace and gracious calling, whether we participate as children of God or rebel as children of the devil. However, it does not add or take away from the completed work of Christ or the redemption won for all humanity on the cross. That is why our lifelong response is the work of the steward and not the owner. That is why grace is truly grace and not merit.

I ask you to hang with me in these next few paragraphs. This understanding of our redemption in Christ as outlined here is critical for our work as steward leaders. We need to be sure we grasp the full nature or what Christ has done for us and what we, as steward leaders, are called to do in response.

We are called and empowered by the Holy Spirit to participate in the redeeming work of Christ through our acceptance of this incredibly gracious act and through our lifelong commitment to steward this precious relationship established for us in Christ Jesus. As we do, we must never, not for one moment, allow this work of stewardship to become solely our work. We cannot act the savior ourselves. We cannot stand on our own before the throne as if it were now our right apart from Christ. Everything that transpires between us and God in this new covenant does so solely through our participation in the already completed work of Christ.

Our relationship to God bears a triune image. This is why we pray to the Father, in the name of and for the sake of the Son, and in the power of the Spirit. That is why our worship is directed to the Father, in the name of the Son and in the Spirit. It is also christocentric—*Christ centered*. It has a direction, calling us to a life of service to God in Christ.

When we talk about being stewards of this first level of relationship with God, broken by our sin and reconciled and restored by the work of Christ, we must speak about it as participation in the work of Christ. This is the work of the godly steward that is attested to throughout Scripture. It is not an autonomous act somehow glued onto our profession of faith, but the one act of accepting what has been done for us in

Christ and participating, through prayer, worship, devotion and service, in the work of the one we now call our Lord and Savior.

Here then is a critical moment for our understanding of the godly steward who is called to lead. Our salvation and our understanding of our call to be stewards are based on our *participation in a gracious act already completed for us.*

This critical truth, in turn, shapes the battle between the two competing views of leading—as stewards or as owners—that operate at all four levels of relationship in which we were created. We can be tempted to fall back into old ways that don't affirm and grasp this amazing priority of grace that ought to permeate our whole life. If we shift our response to these reconciled relationships from joyous to required effort, we move from being a steward to acting as an owner. We shift from being the gracious recipient of a gift to be treasured and stewarded to thinking of ourselves as owners and cocreators with legal rights and the ability to control and use these relationships to our benefit.

Whether it is the understanding of the grace of God for us in Christ, our place and vocation as the creatures of God in this world, our fellowship and communion with our neighbors, or our standing and relationship with God's created world in which we live, our call to be stewards is based on our *acceptance of each as a gracious gift and our rejection of the lure to play the owner.*

Each level was broken by sin and has been redeemed and given back to us in and through Christ Jesus. Each is a gift that needs nothing added to be "complete." Each calls to us to accept this redemption with humility, to participate at each level with joy, and to enter into our call to steward each relationship with gratitude and passion. Each calls for a free and joyous response and not a legal agreement based on mutual conditions and obligations. The prior gracious working of God in Christ serves as the foundation for a theology of the godly steward, and from it flows the calling and work of the steward leader. Everything I have said and will say stands or falls on this point.

On the second level, Christ came to restore our *relationship with our self* and to reclaim for us a holistic understanding of who we are as his children. In Christ we are citizens of his kingdom. Even more we are children of the King! As God's beloved children we have a vocation, a future and a role. We know why we are here, what our purpose is in life and where we are going. That's what it means to be a Christian. All that was lost in the Fall, including our self-perception and worth, has been fully and completely restored to us in Christ.

By redeeming our relationship with God, Jesus offers us back our self-understanding. We can once again know who we are because we know *whose* we are. We can put aside the distortions that sin would inject into our self-awareness, and we can see ourselves—body, mind and spirit—as belonging to the God who created us for fellowship and redeemed us in his Son. Jesus Christ bore our distorted self-image, our egocentrism, our self-hatred, our aimless quest for purpose and our self-delusion. We are now invited back into a right relationship with ourselves through our participation in the ministry of the one who redeemed us and through whom we have access to our Creator. The process of nurturing, strengthening and guarding the relationship we have with ourselves in the power of the Holy Spirit is the work of the godly steward, and the steward leader.

We have also been reconciled in our *relationship with our neighbor.* With the Great Commission, the Great Commandment now calls us back to love one another and to take care of our neighbor. We've been called to the ministry of reconciliation, peacemaking and servanthood. We are able to love our neighbor properly because we can now love ourselves as God's beloved—and redeemed—creation.

By redeeming our relationship to God, Jesus calls us into this right relationship with our neighbor. The enmity and strife that was evidenced immediately in Eden, that was confirmed just as immediately by Cain and that now characterizes so much of our nation and our world was also assumed by Christ. His "becoming flesh" meant his assumption of this discord. His death for the sins of the world meant his overcoming this strife. His resurrection meant that we can now participate in his work of reconciliation. He has taken back our brokenness, assumed it, redeemed it and now calls us to himself to be children in his kingdom, where we are empowered to live in right relationships with our neighbor. Relationships are gifts bought with a precious price and returned to us to be stewarded with obedience and joy.

Finally, we have a *redeemed relationship with creation*. We see ourselves once again as both the "crown of creation" and one with creation. We are again given back our true calling to care for and rule over the world with a loving and godly rule. This impacts our use of time, talents and treasures, and it calls us into a true stewardship relationship with our resources and our environment.

It is in the area of resources and the environment that we struggle the most to retain our true calling as stewards and not owners. Evangelical Christians have been late to the table in this process. For too long they have isolated the redemptive work of Christ to the first level only. It is time to reclaim a more holistic, biblical understanding of Christ's redemptive work, which includes all of creation, "for God was pleased to have all his fullness dwell in him, and through him to reconcile to himself all things, whether things on earth or things in heaven, by making peace through his blood, shed on the cross" (Colossians 1:19-20).

We were created as caretakers of creation, and in Christ we have been restored to that high and holy calling. How else could God's redeemed people respond than to love and care for God's beloved and restored creation? It is simply bad theology that would lead us to believe that God does not care about his creation and so passes on to us the right to exploit and abuse it for our own good. It is equally bad theology to believe that caring for creation is less important to God than other parts of our calling.

There is no hierarchy of responses for the godly steward. Caring for creation does not take a back seat to our other responses as God's redeemed people. It is not a tag-on, done only in our spare time after we have finished doing the more important work of the kingdom. Godly stewards are called to respond to Christ's redemptive work at all four levels. We are either stewards of them all or we fail to be the obedient stewards God created us to be. We fall back and play the owner and the lord when we choose which of our responses is more important or more central to the gospel. God has called us to be obedient stewards on all four levels.

The Godly Steward

What then is holistic stewardship? *We are stewards of our redeemed and restored relationships on all four levels.* According to this definition, we are called first to be stewards of our relationship *with God.* That means that our worship, reading and study of the Scriptures, personal devotions and prayer life are acts of stewardship.

In what ways are you living as a faithful steward of your relationship with God?

How does your time reading God's Word, in prayer and in private devotion reflect a heart of joyful obedience?

How do you assure that your worship time is one of true doxology?

In our redeemed relationship *with ourselves* we are now caretakers of our understanding of who we are as children of the kingdom of God. This is a delicate balance; we are precious and beloved by God but also humble, thankful and obedient to his Word. As we maintain that balance with the help of the Holy Spirit, we are stewards of our self-image.

In what ways are you living as a faithful steward of your relationship with your self?

Do you tend to be pulled toward either pride or self-abasement? Which way and why?

Do you claim today the balance that you can find in Christ?

We are also stewards of our relationships *with our neighbor.* We are called to be in good, whole, right, loving relationships with one another, seeking to love our neighbor as ourselves, working for peace and reconciliation, and serving our neighbors' physical, emotional and spiritual needs as the Spirit directs us. We are called to make sure that our relationships with one another are never *means* but always *ends*.

In what ways are you living as a faithful steward of your relationship with your neighbor?

What action demonstrates that you value your relationship with your neighbor as an end in itself?

What must you do to invest the time necessary to build community and meaningful relationships with others?

Finally, our restored relationship *with creation* calls us to be stewards of God's creation and all the material possessions that we have, placing them and all of God's beloved creation in the service of one kingdom of Christ.

In what ways are you living as a faithful steward of your relationship with God's creation?

Do you pray over decisions on what you buy, consume and use? Why or why not?

What must you do to ensure that you place everything into God's control and seek to be obedient in caring for his creation?

The calling of a steward leader is built on the theology of the godly steward. As such it is a theology of worship as a joyful response to the God who is for us in Jesus Christ. A godly steward is a new creation in Christ. A godly steward is a joyous servant in the kingdom of God. A godly steward is a child of the King. A godly steward has a mission and a purpose in life. A godly steward is one who knows God in real, personal and certain terms, and who knows that God is for us. In all of this, a godly steward is free.

These are the foundations on which we will build an understanding of the unique calling of a steward leader.

2

THE FREEDOM OF
THE STEWARD LEADER

Jesus spoke more frequently about the kingdom of God than any other subject recorded in Scripture. I wonder then why it was not more of a major theme in my own church upbringing. I only stumbled on the importance of the term in seminary when I read John Bright's *The Kingdom of God*. Perhaps for many of us the idea of a kingdom seems like something out of Camelot or Narnia. Yet we cannot deny its central place in Scripture.

Simply put, we are stewards *in God's kingdom*. This new kingdom that has come among us in the work of Christ is complete, yet also transitional. It is complete in that it is the kingdom of the Son, whose work to restore all things is complete. It is transitional in that it has come into this sinful world, which does not know that restoration has been made for it at every level.

The kingdom of this world celebrates the self as king. In seeking to be its own god and thirsting for the control of Eden, the self reenacts the Fall and chooses evil over good again and again. It rebels against grace and therefore chooses destruction over life. It still plays the owner and therefore chooses manipulation, exploitation and abuse over the work of the godly steward.

The kingdom of God has come, and so we see it only in glimpses in the lives of those who have been called into that kingdom, who have repented in the face of grace and who have embraced the role of steward with joy. In Hebrews 2, we see this twofold nature of the kingdom of God in the work of Christ:

> You made him a little lower than the angels; you crowned him with glory and honor and put everything under his feet. In putting everything under him, God left nothing that is not subject to him. Yet at present we do not see everything subject to him. But we see Jesus, who was made a little lower than the angels, now crowned with glory and honor because he suffered death, so that by the grace of God he might taste death for everyone. (Hebrews 2:7-9)

We see Jesus! That is the result of the work of the steward. In a world that sees everything apart from Christ's control, people still can see Jesus in the lives of the workers of his kingdom.

The kingdom of God has come in the work of Christ. God left nothing that is not subject to him. There is nothing that needs to be added to complete the kingdom or to usher it in from some heavenly waiting room. Even in this provisional form, it is here in Christ, and we are the body of Christ!

The evidence of this new kingdom is found in the lives of the people of the kingdom who live as stewards in a world of owners. We proclaim the restoration of all things in Christ. That is the message of the gospel that calls men and women to repentance and wholeness as children in the kingdom of the triune God of grace. We live as ones who have received an invaluable gift: restored relationships at all four levels in Christ. And so we respond by entering into our call to be stewards of these relationships, rejecting the temptation to take control, to add a legal requirement to a gracious gift, to abuse and exploit, to own and put it into service for our own benefit or as an act of a quest for self-actualization.

By accepting this vocation and by rejecting these temptations, we live as children of Christ's kingdom. And as we do, the world around us is given a glimpse of the fact that all things are indeed in subjection to Christ. They are given a glimpse of the true reality of their creaturely existence. They are given a glimpse of what will be revealed in its fullness at the second coming of the Son, when what is now only seen in part will be manifest in all creation. They are given a glimpse of Jesus.

I would call this being a one-kingdom steward. One-kingdom stew-

ards have submitted everything on all four levels to the full authority of
the one Lord who reigns over the one kingdom of God. Everything they
have has been laid at the feet of one Lord in every area of their life. Living
as one-kingdom stewards is their calling, their vocation and their joy.

The Rise of the Second Kingdom

Unfortunately, few of us would claim to be complete, committed, holistic, one-kingdom people. Despite our desire to be totally and solely
committed to Jesus Christ and to give everything to him, we hold back
parts of our lives from God. As we do, we build a second kingdom.

Jesus met this temptation head-on at the outset of his public ministry. The third and final temptation that Satan laid before Jesus following his baptism was the invitation to be lord over his own kingdom,
apart from the kingdom of God:

> Again, the devil took him to a very high mountain and showed him all of
> the kingdoms of the world and their splendor. "All of this I will give you,"
> he said, "if you will bow down and worship me." (Matthew 4:8-9)

Before Jesus could proclaim the coming of the kingdom of God, Satan
offered him a second kingdom of his own.

Jesus rejected this temptation, but if we are honest with ourselves, we
must admit that we all build second kingdoms over which we serve as
lord. They consist of the things over which we seek to maintain control,
such as time, possessions, relationships, reputation and future. At each
of the four levels is a temptation to carve out a place where we can play
the owner and ruler over some aspect of it. And so we build our earthly
kingdoms and rely on them to ascribe to us a large measure of our self-
worth, satisfaction and security.

The last thing in the world that the enemy wants is for you and me
to be completely committed to Jesus Christ. Our enemy shows us, too,
the splendor of kingdoms that he wants to give us and over which we
can play the king. He desperately wants to divert our attention, sow the
seeds of discontent, confuse, deceive and twist the truth just enough so
that we become comfortable with those small compromises that later
grow into major distortions.

I preached a sermon recently in which I used a wooden box to hide what I claimed to be a treasure beyond all imaginable value. I said that in that box was the one item that kings and presidents go to war over, that wealthy and powerful people spend their entire lives pursuing, and that every person in the church that morning would give everything they owned to possess, if even for just a moment.

I turned my back to the congregation, opened the box and revealed the highly coveted item—a magician's wand. But this was no ordinary wand. This one magical device had the power to give to its bearer complete control over any and every area of his life. With it a person could control health and finances, manipulate the stock market, change the outcome of sporting events and determine the weather. The bearer could alter the behavior of others, smite his or her enemies, even the score for all the injustices in life and make things right where he or she had been wronged. The one who used the wand could get a better job, improve the behavior of his or her spouse and kids, buy a bigger house and take a vacation anywhere in the world.

The wand represented the control we so long to have over our life. It is the desire for power, for the ability to shape things so they come out our way, to be the lord of our lives and the people and things that comprise it. We believe that if we just had more control, our life would be better, we could make things come out the way we want and guide our own destiny.

This is the best way I can illustrate second-kingdom building. It is less about our stuff than about our hearts, but it is about our stuff as well. It is the struggle between God's kingdom and a counterfeit earthly kingdom we want to label as "ours." It is ultimately about lordship.

The Battle for the Kingdom

In the sharpest possible distinction, the call to live for Christ is a call to give up *all* things in our earthly kingdom. God has asked us to lay aside those things that are not of his kingdom. German theologian Dietrich Bonhoeffer proclaimed it clearly: "When Christ calls a man, he bids him come and die."[1] So, if you have come to Christ, God has called you to step off the throne and come into his kingdom fully, completely and unreservedly.

When we are called to leadership, the temptation to two-kingdom living grows exponentially. Thus begins one of the greatest spiritual battles of our life. On one hand, the enemy works in us to shift our allegiance to anything but the lordship of Christ. On the other, the Holy Spirit works in us a transformation that empowers us to reject our personal kingdoms and live as one-kingdom people. This process of dismantling and disowning for the sake of trusting and obeying is at the heart of the effective steward leader. It occurs at all four levels, because the enemy wants us to seize control at all four levels. When a person puts everything under the one lordship of Jesus Christ, he or she gives up that control. The call to one-kingdom living is a call to the daily exercise of dying to self and rising to righteousness, of taking up our cross and following him. It is affirming with Paul that "I no longer live, but Christ lives in me" (Galatians 2:20).

This great battle, as the internal work of transformation by the Holy Spirit, cannot be separated from our vocation and calling as leaders. The call to be steward leaders is a wholly transformative one. Our obedient submission to its transforming power determines the effectiveness of our work. Both the calling and the function of a steward leader are based on this transformation.

This work is our vocation as steward leaders. Yet the very term *vocation* may be misleading. We most commonly use it to denote *our* efforts, the employment of *our* skills and the reliance on *our* experience. In the tension of being and doing, the study of leadership is almost completely stacked on the doing side. Even when the character and values of the leader are taken seriously (in both secular and faith-based studies), they are most often valued only as they relate to and contribute to the "success" of the leader. That is, the measurable outcomes of leadership dictate the level of importance placed on the inward life of the leader.

I will use the term *vocation* in a different way, defining vocation for a steward leader as "obedient and joyful response." Throughout Scripture, God "called" leaders, asking only for their obedient response. He called many ill-equipped, untrained, dysfunctional, poorly skilled men and women into leadership. He thrust them into impossible situations with recalcitrant people and asked only that they be obedient and trusting. This is the posture of the one-kingdom steward leader.

Such stewards understand that the relationships they enjoy at all four levels are gifts from God. Each was part of God's rich and wondrous intent for us at creation. Each was lost through our own sinfulness. And each has been restored to us through the blood of Christ. So expensive a gift as this now demands our faithful stewarding. But that work is still not wholly ours, for it is the result of the ongoing work of transformation that the Spirit accomplishes in each of us who will respond obediently to our calling.

If this is true for us as godly stewards, it is true for us in our work as leaders. Thus the term "steward leader." *Our vocation is a participation in the transforming work God is doing in us, and it is a process of letting that work transform us as leaders, the people we serve and the organizations we lead.*

Becoming a steward leader does not require that you learn another set of techniques. There are no "Twelve Steps to Becoming an Effective Steward Leader." You cannot take a course in it, get a certificate for it or read a book and apply it. It is a vocation that demands unequivocal obedience and wholehearted response. However, precisely because it requires this *and nothing more,* it is a vocation of freedom. We are freed from the reliance on techniques or charm or charisma or leadership self-help programs. We are freed from both nature (being born to lead) and nurture (having to learn the skills as we go).

This is not to say that we do not apply all that God has given to us. It is also not to say that we do not learn and grow, read and acquire skills to help us be the best leaders we can. The fundamental understanding here is that, despite what we might bring to the job or learn on the job, we are called to a transforming, obedient response to the vocation of the steward leader.

The One Calling of the Steward Leader

Obedient and joyful response—that is the only requirement of the steward leader. However, for us to be true to this calling, to be consistent and unshakable in this one vocational focus, we must embrace a new paradigm for effective leadership. This paradigm emphasizes "being" over "doing" and freedom over ownership.

Recapturing the joy of being. "We are continually tempted to forget that it is not what men *do* that is the vital matter, but rather what they *are*. In Jesus Christ neither legal observances nor the omission of legal observances avails anything, 'but a new creature.' God is a great deal more concerned about our really *being* new creatures than about anything else; because he knows that if we *are* right as to our inward being, we shall certainly *do* right as to our outward actions. . . . The essential thing, therefore, is character; and *doing* is valuable only as it is an indication of 'being.'"[2]

These words from Hannah Whitehall Smith's classic *The Christian's Secret to a Happy Life* illustrate the foundational principle for the steward leader. Scripture speaks clearly and directly to this theme. Throughout the message of God's saving work in Jesus Christ, we learn that God seeks first the transformation of our hearts before the transaction of our business. Matthew records,

> From that time on Jesus began to explain to his disciples that he must go to Jerusalem and suffer many things at the hands of the elders, chief priests and teachers of the law, and that he must be killed and on the third day be raised to life.
>
> Peter took him aside and began to rebuke him. "Never, Lord!" he said. "This shall never happen to you!"
>
> Jesus turned and said to Peter, "Get behind me, Satan! You are a stumbling block to me; you do not have in mind the things of God, but the things of men."
>
> Then Jesus said to his disciples, "If anyone would come after me, he must deny himself and take up his cross and follow me. For whoever wants to save his life will lose it, but whoever loses his life for me will find it. What good will it be for a man if he gains the whole world, yet forfeits his soul? Or what can a man give in exchange for his soul?" (Matthew 16:21-26)

The denial of self for the sake of the cross does not mean that we set aside self-care or deny ourselves the time we need for spiritual growth. The life we are called to lose is precisely the doing-driven life that measures worth by accomplishments and wealth by possessions and power.

We are called to lose the life that promises applause and material reward, that we might be given the true life of the godly steward. Jesus makes it clear by asking what the value of a life of doing—gaining the whole world—is if it costs us our very being—forfeiting our soul. Being a godly steward of our self has an internal, transformation focus rather than an external, transaction focus. It is life versus death, fulfillment versus burnout, freedom versus bondage.

In his letter to the church in Corinth, Paul writes,

> If I speak in the tongues of men and of angels, but have not love, I am only a resounding gong or a clanging cymbal. If I have the gift of prophecy and can fathom all mysteries and all knowledge, and if I have a faith that can move mountains, but have not love, I am nothing. If I give all I possess to the poor and surrender my body to the flames, but have not love, I gain nothing. (1 Corinthians 13:1-3)

Paul points to the transformation of the heart as the normative and requisite transformation from which all our acts of love must flow. Cut off from inner transformation, our acts, our very best doing, is reduced to "a resounding gong or a clanging cymbal." It profits us nothing. *We* are nothing. It is empty and void of meaning.

Compare the following two stories from Matthew:

> Now a man came up to Jesus and asked, "Teacher, what good thing must I do to get eternal life?"
>
> "Why do you ask me about what is good?" Jesus replied. "There is only One who is good. If you want to enter life, obey the commandments."
>
> "Which ones?" the man inquired.
>
> Jesus replied, "'Do not murder, do not commit adultery, do not steal, do not give false testimony, honor your father and mother,' and 'love your neighbor as yourself.'"
>
> "All these I have kept," the young man said. "What do I still lack?"
>
> Jesus answered, "If you want to be perfect, go, sell your possessions and give to the poor, and you will have treasure in heaven. Then come, follow me."
>
> When the young man heard this, he went away sad, because he had great wealth. (Matthew 19:16-22)

"The kingdom of heaven is like treasure hidden in a field. When a man found it, he hid it again, and then in his joy went and sold all he had and bought that field." (Matthew 13:44)

The contrast of these two Scriptures is striking. Both speak of the transformation of the heart and how it impacts our actions. In the first, the rich young ruler asks what he must *do* to inherit eternal life. He asks Jesus a two-kingdom question, and Jesus gives him a one-kingdom answer. It is not about doing, but being. It requires a change of heart, which was too much to ask for the wealthy inquisitor. He went away in his two-kingdom mindset, trying to *do* his way into the kingdom of God. And all it brought him was sadness.

Jesus also tells us the story of a man who was plowing his field and came across a treasure of great price. Presumably it was no less valuable than the entrance into the kingdom of God sought by the rich young ruler. However, the farmer has a change of heart, a *metanoia,* and that translates into changed action. He not only does what the rich young ruler cannot—sell his possessions—but he does it with great joy.

One person was given an opportunity to set aside his kingdom-building bondage to walk with Jesus in freedom, and he went away sad. The other realized the unparalleled wealth of the kingdom of God and joyfully sold everything he had to answer its call. He was free!

We live in an incredible tension between being and doing. So let me ask you the following questions.

What criteria do you use when you allocate your time and talents?

What drives your daily schedule, your personal goals?

What determines your vocational satisfaction?

What fills your deepest need for acceptance, meaning and self-worth?

Are your responses tied to the person you are and are becoming in Christ, or to what you have accomplished? Is your self-worth tied to the quality of your being or the quantity of your doing? I am not saying that our doing is not important, even necessary and commanded by God for the building of his kingdom. The question is not about the relative importance of our doing God's work, but a matter of priority. Our being is foundational, and our doing is built upon it.

I acknowledge that there is circularity to this process: our faithful work for the kingdom nurtures our being, strengthens our faith and prepares us for even greater obedience and service. In his book *Leading People from the Middle*, Whitworth University president Bill Robinson states that "our behavior changes to the extent that our beliefs, attitudes, intentions, experience and environment propel the change."[3] Being without doing cannot bring about transformation in our life. The two are integrally linked and equally necessary for our development.

The predominant temptation of leaders today, however, is certainly not an overemphasis on being. We are doing ourselves to death. When the drive to succeed is rooted in a sense that we own our ministry, own our employees and own our vision, leadership consumes us. Vocational burnout and the moral failures that plague our country and the church are not the result of too much focus on our spiritual health and transformation into the likeness of Christ. Instead, they are symptoms of a view of leadership that places value almost exclusively on what we accomplish, regardless of the consequences for us and those around us.

Fortunately, leadership studies—both faith-based and secular—are focusing much attention on the inner being of the leader as a key component to leadership success. The world (and the church) is waking up to the reality that inner character influences a person's effectiveness as a leader. Yet the remedies offered often throw us back on ourselves to somehow develop more integrity or nurture greater inner spiritual strength in order to be better leaders. Notice that the work is still ours, and therefore our doing is still the necessary thing. The lure of self-reliance is insidious throughout leadership studies. We're attempting to heal our very being, but this is no cure.

When we say that God is more concerned with who we are than what we do, we acknowledge that God's work of transformation in us is his first priority. We also acknowledge that it must remain his work, with our vital and only role being to live as an open and obedient vessel for this work. Even here we must be careful not to make this our work. Our action is only response to the work God has completed for us in Christ. So we humbly and joyously await and welcome the Holy Spirit, who graciously works to transform us into the godly stewards, and steward leaders, we were created to be.

I cannot emphasize enough how important this priority of being over doing is if we are to be used by God to lead. It goes against so much of what we experience in leadership roles. It demands that we not only set aside time to nurture our spirit, but that we give priority and value to this time. Even if we manage to set aside this time and religiously adhere to it, we still may come away feeling guilty for investing precious time in something that seems so self-serving and nonproductive. Leaders are measured by reaching goals, achieving growth and improving the bottom line, so we must fight for an acceptance of being over doing. This is an internal fight as much as an organizational fight, and it is one we must win at both levels if we are to be true to our calling as steward leaders.

I sat at lunch with a beleaguered pastor who told me the story of his need for a day for spiritual preparation and growth. His congregation gave him only one day off each week and expected him to be in his office or making calls the other five, and of course, to preach and visit church families on Sunday.

He had written out a carefully scripted case for his need for a day when he would take no calls and see no parishioners, but would dedicate himself to Bible study, prayer and personal preparation for the challenges of leading the congregation. The church board met and read his letter. As they prepared to discuss his request, the board chairperson rose and said, "We will now entertain questions and comments regarding the pastor's request for another day off." His church simply could not value time given to help their pastor grow as a child of God.

If we seek to shift the paradigms in our organizations, we will face a conflict of values and expectations set more by the world than by its Creator. Yet we must enter this conflict and win it. It is the root of our survival and, more importantly, of our obedience as steward leaders.

Israel Gaither, Commander of the Salvation Army, shared this story with me:

It was August 2006. My wife and I were preparing to return to the USA from an overseas assignment in a developing sector of the world, to take up senior-level leadership positions in the organization in which we both serve. For several months prior to our actual arrival, while in preparation of my mind and heart, the Lord gave me a strong vision to cast for the movement. The direction of the Lord not only excited me, it gripped me!

Within a very short time after taking up our new duties, I had the opportunity to convey the vision to about two thousand who are associated with the movement. I laid out the dream God gave me, and it was enthusiastically accepted, confirming that not only had I arrived in the responsibility at the right time, but the vision given to me was of the Lord.

But a few weeks later the bubble burst! Our organization underwent a change at the highest level of our international movement, and the result of that process, to my surprise, meant that my wife and I would once again be called to leave America to assume an even greater leadership responsibility on the international scene. While the appointment affirmed my gifts and skills, it seemed all wrong that God would give me a strong vision for organizational expansion and growth, and then so quickly take it from me by asking me (after just three months) to move on to another overseas assignment. I was devastated.

But I learned the meaning of "being."

I struggled for several days and finally decided that not another day must pass without knowing that it was God who willed that I should take the next assignment. It was early Sunday morning, and as I prayed, read Scripture and reflected, the Holy Spirit challenged me with the reminder that I was called to serve His ideas—they were not mine. I was a steward, and not in control of the timing of His purposes. I suddenly realized that God had me where He wanted me for "His time," not mine. He had provided the vision for "His purposes," not mine. It was about "Him," not "me."

My business was to "be" obedient to His call on my life. Although it was a spiritually and emotionally draining experience, that lesson will never be lost on me.

The one calling of the steward leader is joyful obedience. This response is always joyful because it springs from a heart that is free. The first step in that response is valuing the work God is seeking to do *in* you more than the work he will do *through* you. We were created to reflect the image of God, and we do that not by our actions primarily, but by our character. We understand that in order to walk the path of the steward leader, we must love before we can serve, follow before we can lead, submit before we can succeed. God's bottom line for you and me as steward leaders is measured in terms of surrender, obedience, transformation and love. My colleague John Savage says, "It's not who you are leading, but who is leading you that matters."

If you will agree that God is more concerned with who you are than with what you do, it will start you down the road of your transformation as a godly steward and a steward leader.

Freed to lead. There has been an ongoing debate in leadership studies regarding whether leaders are born or made. The nature-versus-nurture discussion has focused on the traits of successful leaders and asked whether these are inherent in the DNA or acquired by those who have learned and plied the skills more successfully than others.

A primary thesis of this book is that God *frees us* to be steward leaders. That freedom is wholly transformative and summons from us obedient response. That obedient response determines the effectiveness of our work. Both the calling and the function of a steward leader are based on this transformation. I, therefore, contend that a steward leader is neither born nor made, but is *freed*.

What frees us is the truth. Jesus said, "If you hold to my teaching, you are really my disciples. Then you will know the truth, and the truth will set you free" (John 8:31). It is the truth of the God revealed to us in Jesus Christ that sets us free. In Christ we learn the truth about God, the truth about ourselves and the truth about our purpose and vocation. In Christ we see lies and deception for what they are, and we respond with obedient joy. Jesus Christ is the truth that sets us free. "So if the Son sets you free, you will be free indeed" (John 8:36).

The conclusion to all I have said so far is simply this: steward leaders are freed to lead. As we are being transformed into godly stewards, we are freed to fulfill our vocation as steward leaders. It is God's calling, Christ's redemption and the Holy Spirit's transformation that we rely on for our success. In this way, leadership is a work of our triune God in us and through us. And if it is God's work, and we are called to obediently respond, then we are freed to lead courageously and humbly, and to trust God for the increase.

Just as we were created to bear the image of God on four levels, so we are freed to lead as godly stewards on those same four levels. Yet this freedom does not come easy. Our enemy wants nothing more than to enslave us again to a bondage that will rob us of all we have gained. Robinson writes,

> In this journey toward freedom, we must remember that remaining in a place of freedom doesn't just happen. The enemy is forever trying to thwart God's best plan for your life through temptation and the lure of "something better." Once we taste freedom, we must understand that the only way to remain in that place is through the disciplined practice of spending time deepening our relationship with God.[4]

For the steward leader, bondage comes in a desire to forsake the freedom of the steward for the lure of absolute ownership. It may seem strange at first to oppose freedom with ownership, but that is exactly the battle we face. Ownership here means a thirst for control, for power and, ultimately, for lordship. Freedom requires humility and trust; ownership sings to us that we are indispensable, that we have all the answers and that our organization could not live without us.

This must be seen clearly for what it is: it is a lie of the enemy that stands directly opposed to the truth of God. The life of a steward leader is a battle for truth. On one side is the revelation of truth given to us in Jesus Christ—the truth about our God, about our own nature, about our calling, our vocation and our future. It is a thoroughly triune-centered worldview, and it is the absolute truth. On the other side is the enemy's deception that began in Eden with "Did God really say . . . ?" and continues to whisper to us every day. It is the lie that God's nature is different from what is revealed to us in Jesus Christ. It is the lie that we are somehow more or less than what God created us to be. It is the lie that our neighbor is there to be used by us to get what we want. And it is the lie that creation, its resources and its beauty are there for us to use for our own pleasure to its ultimate destruction.

Steward leaders are truth tellers, because they know the truth that has set them free. This truth is not a teaching, a religion, a lifestyle or a worldview. It is not an interpretation, a spiritual journey or a model to follow. This truth is not a "what" in any shape or form. The truth that sets us free is a "who." Scripture makes this abundantly clear.

> I am the way the truth and the life. (John 14:6)

> We have seen his glory, the glory of the One and Only, who came from the Father, full of grace and truth. (John 1:14)

> For this reason I was born, and for this I came into the world, to testify to the truth. (John 18:37)

> You shall know the truth, and the truth shall set you free. . . . If the Son sets you free you will be free indeed. (John 8:32, 36)

Freedom in the truth that is Christ or bondage in the lies of the enemy—that is the choice set before us. Ownership is bondage born of lies, pure and simple. We see it worked out on the four levels at which we are invited to live as the free stewards of the triune God of grace. Our freedom, and the temptation to the bondage of ownership, is as holistic as the calling of a godly steward.

We are free then, first in our *relationship with God*. We respond to his grace and love through our free and spontaneous expressions of worship, praise, prayer, devotion and vocation. He has set us free for such a free response. "It was for freedom that Christ has set us free" (Galatians 5:1). This freedom brings deep loyalty without obligation. We do not love God *in order to* be loved by him, but "we love him because he first loved us" (1 John 4:19). We are freed to respond and are cut loose from any sense of duty, obligation or guilt-induced ritual. It is not the wrath of God that forces us; "Christ's love compels us" (2 Corinthians 5:14). At this first level, we must hold firmly to the conviction that we are free in our relationship to God, and as his stewards we respond in joy.

The enemy, however, distorts the free response of grace into a duty that we must carry out in allegiance to God. When our response to grace becomes an obligation, we are again thrown back on ourselves to perform. This is burdensome and robs us of the joy of the obedient steward. But it is much more heinous than that. In turning gracious response into burdensome duty, the enemy has also put us in control of our relationship with God. And with control comes a sense of ownership. Once we believe that we control our relationship with God, we have been had. We begin to worship out of guilt. We become legalistic about our devotional time. When we read Scripture, we do it impatiently, always looking for a key verse that we can use productively. Gone is the joy of worship, the intimacy of devotional time in the presence of the Spirit and the meditation on Scripture just for the sake of communing with the Word of God.

The shift from the joyful and free response of the steward to the burdened response of the owner is subtle. We can slip slowly from one to the other without noticing it. This is why the vocation of the godly steward requires diligence. It is a battle for our soul that we fight every day in the power of the Spirit.

As godly stewards, we are also free in our *relationship with our self.* As stewards of our self-perceptions, we can see ourselves as God sees us and remain in the balance between our need for daily forgiveness and our identity as beloved children of God. Humility and courage can resound in our spirit if we are free toward ourselves to know who we are in Christ and to be secure in our place as a child of his kingdom. This freedom is an incredibly powerful gift. It keeps us from needing constantly to try to prove our worth on the one hand and doubting it on the other.

Again, the enemy wants to steal this joy from us and replace our freedom with bondage to the preservation of our reputation and to the frantic protection and reclamation of our self-image. If we believe that we are the owners, and therefore the guardians, of our reputation, we will be ensnared in an endless pursuit of trying to prove ourselves to be right, seeking our vindication and righting every wrong that has been done to us. In the same way, if our self-image can be shaken by the response of others, we will respond as owners and face the constant need to prop up our self-worth or bring down that of others around us.

This is a frenetic and unsettled way to live, but it is the only possible life when we shift from steward to owner of our self-perception.

Our self-worth has depth and stability as it is anchored in Christ and his love for us. When this love and acceptance become the unshakable foundation for our self-understanding, we are truly freed to serve the kingdom as steward leaders.

We are also freed in our *relationship with our neighbor*. We can consider our neighbors' needs, work for their well-being, rejoice in their victories, challenge them when they go astray and embrace them when they fall. We are freed from the need to be over and against our neighbors, to put ourselves in a place above them, to benefit from their misfortunes or to be threatened by their accomplishments. And when we are freed in this way toward our neighbors, we can be granted by them the awesome privilege of leading them.

Here the enemy wants so desperately to rob us of our freedom toward the people with whom we live and work. He beckons us to see every relationship as a way to meet our own needs. When he succeeds in reshaping our perceptions of those around us so that we focus on what they can do for us, he has succeeded in cultivating in us an owner's heart.

The Arbinger Institute published a fascinating book titled *Leadership and Self-Deception*. It is the story of a new employee of a unique business and his process of discovering the corporate value system of being "out of the box" toward one another. This concept of being out of the box toward others is synonymous with the freedom a steward leader has toward his or her people. Consider the following discussion of leaders who are "inside the box":

> They run all over people, trying to get only their own results with devastating effects. They might beat their chests and preach, focusing on results, but it's a lie. In the box, they—like everyone else—are focused on themselves. But in the box, they—like everyone else—can't see it because when I'm blaming them, I'm not doing it because they need to improve. I'm blaming them because their shortcomings justify my failure to improve. People who came together to help an organization suc-

ceed actually end up delighting in each other's failures and resenting each other's successes.[5]

This is a splendid example of the owner-leader. Owners see relationships for what they can produce. People are used and manipulated to achieve the owner's ends. But this statement is too sharp; the shift can be subtle. We can simply view people as needing us. Our employees depend on us, our colleagues rely on our skills, our spouse cannot live without us. And so we respond as any owner would. We nurture that dependence, capitalize on the reliance and broker the love for personal gains.

Later in *Leadership and Self-Deception,* the fictional character, Lou, describes the pivotal moment in his own self-reflection:

> I saw in myself a leader who was so sure of the brilliance of his own ideas that he couldn't allow brilliance in anyone else's. A leader who felt he was so enlightened, that he needed to see workers negatively in order to prove his enlightenment. A leader so driven to be the best, that he made sure no one else could be as good as he was.[6]

What would it mean for you to be truly free in your relationships with the people around you? What would it mean to allow each person to be fully the person God created him or her to be—and for you to be used by God to help each be that person? What if we operated in all our relationships as if there was nothing in them for us, but focused all our energy on the well-being of others?

We have been freed for such a role in this world, one that is transformative. It is radical and it is the free response of the godly steward who is called to lead.

Finally, we are freed in our *relationship with the creation.* We no longer need to hoard resources or amass possessions to build our own kingdom. We can live lightly in this world, caring for our environment, giving freely and joyously, holding loosely to the trappings of success and trusting God to meet our needs regardless of the circumstances. This is real freedom. It acknowledges that God is the owner of all things, and it goes further in affirming that "God will meet all your needs according to his glorious riches in Christ Jesus" (Philippians 4:19). To be free toward creation means we ask the steward question first and the personal-gain question second (or never!). Every decision we make impacts this world, and we are freed to ask what actions best preserve this creation, believing that God seeks only our obedient response.

The enemy despises such freedom and works to coax us to place some level of dependence on anything other than the love and grace of Christ—our possessions, our retirement plans, our income, our assets or our accomplishments. He wants us to put our trust in a job, a stock portfolio, a paid-off mortgage or a future inheritance. But when we play the owner of our assets, we shift our dependence onto something other than God. For a leader of a not-for-profit, this may be an endowment, a major supporter, or a grant from a foundation. For a business leader, it may be the profits from a new product or the promise of a new sales manager. For pastors, our dependence may rest on a growing membership or a new associate.

As owners we must constantly work to protect our assets and promote growth. It is up to us to cast vision, plan strategically and lead boldly. None of these ideas are wrong if they are carried out as the obedient response of a steward leader who has taken them on freely and joyfully. However, when they are the actions of an owner-leader, they become an anxious grasping at a future that the leader believes he or she must make happen. So it becomes *his or her* vision, *his or her* strategic plan. The leader owns it, and it reciprocates by drowning him or her in an anxious pursuit of its achievement.

Steward leaders must never fall to the temptation to make God's vision their own. They are stewards of the vision God reveals to his people. Because it is God's *vision*, steward leaders respond with a passionate obedience to its calling. And because it is *God's* vision, they do so in a freedom that brings fulfillment and joy.

On the cover of this book is a picture of a soaring bald eagle. It was chosen because it is a symbol of freedom. Many times I have sat at my desk in Spokane buried with work and sensing the stress level increase, only to look out and see two bald eagles soaring high above the Little Spokane River near our home. As I watched them I envied their sense of freedom. Even though they relied daily on the provision of food from the earth, they never looked hurried. They spread their magnificent wings to catch the thermals of the warm afternoon and seemed to soar higher and higher just for the fun of doing it. They are perfectly equipped for their role in the ecosystem. To me they have both a majestic and a humble presence in the skies. As I think about the steward leader, I am led to the image of this great bird that is both free to soar and also created for a distinct purpose within God's wonderful creation. Free and purposeful. Humble and majestic. What a beautiful symbol.

Would you like to know this radical freedom as a godly steward? Would you like to lead your organizations with that same sense of freedom—toward yourself, your colleagues, your finances, your mission and future? A combination of freedom and joyful obedience is the defining mark of the steward leader. Steward leaders are neither born nor made; they are freed for this work.

3

THE DISTINCTIVENESS OF
THE STEWARD LEADER

This chapter is not intended to be an exhaustive survey and comparison of secular and faith-based leadership theories. Its intent is to create the context and frame the key questions at the heart of the contemporary leadership debate within the community of believers in Jesus Christ. My purpose is to frame the question of how the theology behind the steward leader is distinct from and also built upon and related to the work that has come before it.

To do this I will compare and contrast a few key representatives in both the secular and the faith-based approaches to leadership.

Secular Leadership Studies

Let's begin by considering several models of leadership—the Great Man theory of leadership, Transactional Leadership, Transformational Leadership and Servant Leadership—and identify their key differences from the Steward Leader model.[1]

Great Man and Charismatic Leadership. The Great Man theory of leadership states that a great leader is born with the traits and character necessary to "bend history's course to his own will."[2] It is a traits-based approach to understanding why some leaders are simply "eventful" while others are "event-making." The moral flaws of great leaders have rendered this theory an unsatisfactory method for defining effective leadership. It was the "who" question that undermined the greatness of the accomplishments of men like Napoleon, Hitler and Stalin—all powerful leaders but scarcely the models you would want to lift up or emulate.

This theory was developed further by Max Weber in the 1920s as Charismatic Leadership, which rests on devotion to the sanctity, heroism or exceptional character of an individual person, and on the normative patterns or order revealed and ordained by him. The emphasis was on the character and innate skills of the leader but added an almost divine component that endowed the leader with the ability to bring about remarkable change not only in circumstances but also within the hearts and attitudes of his followers.

The charismatic leader is rare, and almost entirely driven by the strength of his or her personality. Some of the ethical collapses witnessed in our most trusted leaders can be traced to the limitations of this type of leadership, including a lack of accountability and a tendency toward narcissism. A charismatic personality may have the hardest time embracing the call to be a steward leader, though he or she may be the type of leader who needs it the most.

Transactional Leadership. The Transactional Leadership theory is based on a mechanistic view of the world that emerged from the scientific worldview of the Enlightenment. It believes that all nature can be dissected and understood as series of causes and effects, including human organizations. Therefore, leaders must successfully negotiate a series of causal transactions that bring about the desired organizational effect. Transactional leadership is a low-risk pursuit of limited but clear goals. Transactional leaders are brokers, coalition formers and consensus builders. They bargain with their followers for mutually beneficial actions. Their focus is on managing public opinion through a series of negotiated actions that please both the leader and the followers.

This is similar to a related theory called the Leader-Member Exchange, which placed leaders in the position of enacting quid pro quo instead of leading with vision. The transactional leader has something the people want and, reciprocally, needs something the people have. So transactions are undertaken and value is exchanged. The value may be power for the people and applause for the leader. It may also be power for the leader in exchange for opportunity for the people. In whatever form, transactional leadership is based on this exchange of valued commodities.

Ministry leaders can fall into transactional leadership with surprising ease. Leaders who seek public favor will watch the direction of the wind and lead accordingly. Give the people what they want, and you will have their love and support—at least temporarily. There is no inner transformation required of the transactional leader. Nor is there any desire or need for the transformation of the people he or she leads. Yet something that sounds so far from the transformed heart of a steward leader remains so very near to our need as leaders to be loved and accepted by the people we lead.

As leaders, by definition we have power. As soon as we use that power as a bargaining chip to get what we want from our people, we become the transactional leader. This understanding of transactional leadership illustrates the important link between a leader's character and his actions. Power leads to transactional behavior when there is no controlling center to guide it in another direction. That is why ongoing transformation of the heart is the fundamental characteristic of the steward leader.

Transformational Leadership. James MacGregor Burns, the father of twentieth-century leadership theory, developed the Transformational Leadership theory. Burns sought to define effective leadership by making a distinction between transformation and change. Change is the product of transactional leadership brought about by an exchange of value. Transformation, on the other hand, is "a basic alteration in entire systems."[3] This basic alteration comes through empowerment. According to Burns, "Instead of exercising power over people, transforming leaders champion and inspire followers." The result is, "people can transform themselves."[4] This is done by reconnecting people to the fundamental values that define their society and shaping change, or reframing those values.

Burns writes that "transforming values lie at the heart of transforming leadership, determining whether leadership indeed can be transforming."[5] For transformation to take place, there must be a connection between leader and follower around a common need for a change according to their wants, discontents and hopes. Transformational leaders must be able to alter the world, not just the values of their people, and give them hope that their current status can be transcended.[6]

Leadership and the new science. Building on Burns's work, Margaret Wheatley has provided a provocative and, in my opinion, very valuable conception of leadership by focusing on applying the changes in the science of physics to a rethinking of organizational life. Wheatley dismisses the mechanistic view of human dynamics in favor of an organic view that understands that values and freedom of choice are stronger determinants of human activity and, therefore, of organizational efficiency. Her work has far more implications for leadership than I can cover here, but we will benefit from making a modest investment of our time with her.

Let me offer a succinct summary of her main point. Quantum physics is radically reshaping our understanding of the physical world. It is causing a shift away from the mechanistic view of Newton to a highly organic, interconnected understanding of the basic components that make up atoms and molecules. Wheatley writes, "In a quantum world, relationships are not just interesting; to many physicists, they are all there is to reality."[7]

Wheatley paints a picture of effective leadership that is able to "dance" with the changes inherent in an organization based on the flux and flow of relationships. Such a leader provides freedom to his or her followers, believing that when people are freed, they will self-organize in ever more effective ways—a lesson learned from quantum physics. "All life lives off-balance in a world that is open to change. And all of life is self-organizing. We do not have to fear disequilibrium, nor do we have to approach change so fearfully."

She goes on to warn us: "When leaders strive for equilibrium and stability by imposing control, constricting people's freedom and inhibiting local change, they only create the conditions that threaten the organization's survival."[8]

Only leaders who are free from the need to "strive for equilibrium and stability" can lead such a process. This is a further step from Burn's idea of transformational leadership, for here the change comes through the free interaction of the people in an evolving relationship that is allowed to self-organize. It requires a leader who is comfortable with ambiguity and free to allow this change to occur without any idea of where it is going or exactly how it will turn out. The leader's role is to articulate and inculcate the values of the organization, so that as it navigates its way through chaotic times, it has these values set as its guide.

> When chaos has banged down the door and is tossing us around the room, it is difficult to believe that clear principles are sufficient. . . . If we can trust the workings of the world, we will see that the strength of our organizations is maintained if we retain clarity about the purpose and direction of the organization. When things become chaotic, this clarity keeps us on course.

Wheatley describes the role of the leader in the midst of this chaos.

> In this chaotic world, we need leaders. But we don't need bosses. We need leaders to help us develop the clear identity that lights the dark moments of confusion. We need leaders to support us as we learn how to live by our values. We need leaders to understand that we are best controlled by concepts that invite our participation, not policies and procedures that curtail our contribution.

Wheatley continues:

> The leader's task is first to embody these principles, and then to help the organization become the standard it has declared for itself. This work of leaders cannot be reversed, or either step ignored.[9]

The embodiment of principles is the highest calling of a leader, according to Wheatley. We will see, unfortunately, that she offers no normative source for these principles. At best they flow from a humanistic belief in the basic goodness of humanity. This is a fatal flaw that ultimately undermines so much of the good work Wheatley has done. However, I don't want to miss her incredibly helpful construct of an organization as fundamentally relational, evolving and held together by unseen forces.[10]

Servant Leadership. Servant Leadership, as espoused by its framer, Robert Greenleaf, is a philosophy of leadership that many have attempted to quantify into lists of characteristics that range from four to eleven, depending on who you read. These include (1) altruistic calling:

the decision to serve others above self, (2) emotional healing: a readiness to listen and to respond to bring about emotional/spiritual recovery, (3) wisdom: an awareness of one's surroundings and an ability to see the convergence of multiple factors, (4) persuasive mapping: seeing the grand vistas and inspiring others to journey toward them, and (5) organizational stewardship: care of the organization and its assets to build the greater good.

According to Greenleaf, servant leadership "begins with the natural feeling that one wants to serve, to serve *first*. Then conscious choice brings one to aspire to lead." The difference between servant-first and leader-first styles of leadership is "the care taken by the servant-first to make sure that other people's highest priority needs are being served."[11]

Servant leaders are distinguished as well by their inclination to seek solutions to the problems of the world by looking first "in here," inside oneself, and then "out there." Servant leaders seek personal change before they seek to change circumstances around them. Greenleaf admits that there is no way to tell who is a servant and who is not. Yet he concludes that the only thing that counts is that "able servants with the potential to lead will lead."[12]

In addition to these writers, we could add the work of Tom Peters, Stephen Covey, Jim Collins and many others who have made significant contributions to this field. The following comparison with my formulation of the steward leader would apply to their work as well as the works cited here.

Comparisons and Contrasts

While not exhaustive, this brief outline of primary theories frames the key questions of leadership and highlights the distinctive features of the steward-leader approach.

A difference of direction. The first and perhaps most fundamental distinction is that these leadership approaches start with a construct for successful leadership and from there seek to identify the traits required of such leadership. I have been very careful not to use the term "steward leader*ship*," because my formulation of the steward leader cannot be reduced to a general theory nor does it offer a specific set of static, measurable traits. My focus in this book is on the person of the steward leader in relationship. How the steward leader leads will vary significantly according to individual personality and giftedness, and the environment, organizational culture, specific challenges and vision into which he or she is called to lead. Most importantly, this leadership is influenced by the work of the Holy Spirit in the heart of the steward leader and his or her responsiveness to that leading in every situation. For that reason I will not talk about traits of leadership, but focus on the heart and dynamic journey of the steward leader.

This relational focus is a significant departure from secular leadership studies, which start with effective leadership and look back to find the traits necessary to bring it about. The Great Man or Charismatic Leadership theory keys on the inherent traits of charisma and vision. The Transactional Leadership theory is geared to a series of transactions dependent on the skills of the leader. Transformational Leadership regards effective leadership as primarily bringing about change in an organization. Servant Leadership sees effective leadership requiring the service of the institution and its people in order to be successful. In each case the model is built on what we *do* to be successful. Each focuses on the skills, traits, aptitude, natural abilities or character of the individual leader that brings about "success."

The steward leader model starts with God's call for us to be godly stewards and then asks what the work of the godly steward looks like when it is lived out in the life of one who is called to lead. The steward leader does not derive her identity from being a leader, even being a steward leader, but solely from being a godly and faithful steward. So, we do not start with leadership as the focus of study; instead, we start with the call from God, independent of individual traits, to be a godly steward. Leadership is only one dimension of the outworking of the life of faith and obedience as a steward under the call of God. Even the servant leadership model begins with leadership and ends with servanthood. The steward leader starts with the call to be a godly steward and ends with the heart of the godly steward, open to transformation, called to lead.

To understand why this is so important we must return to the question of being versus doing. I offered earlier the idea that who we are is more important to God than what we do. Our transformation into godly stewards is the *modus operandi* of the kingdom of God. The term *steward* is a descriptor of who we are. Stewards obey, and steward leaders are called to obedient and joyful response.

This response is an indication that steward leaders do not act independently out of their own resources. Their actions are not their own. They are connected to their source, directed by their master and wholly dependent on their savior. In this way the steward leader does not put confidence in innate goodness or giftedness in order to act benevolently. Quite the opposite. Steward leaders understand their complete and utter reliance on God as the source of the goodness, wisdom and justice to which they are called.

A difference of philosophy. The second distinction lies at a more philosophical level: the root belief that produces the direction and content of each of the leadership theories. These theories depend on a secular humanist belief that there is a basic goodness to human nature that most successful leaders have tapped into. Indeed, the belief in the basic goodness of the autonomous human spirit and its inherent capacity to draw from that goodness consistently and reliably is the philosophical basis for every influential non-faith-based theory of leadership that was developed throughout the twentieth century.

In assessing leadership studies, we see a basic conflict between this sense of innate goodness and the Christian doctrine of original sin. It is the conflict between the idea of the pursuit of happiness and what I will call the pursuit of faithfulness. To illuminate this comparison, I will return briefly to Burns's Transformational Leadership, Wheatley's groundbreaking work on leadership and the new science, and Greenleaf's Servant Leadership.

Transformational leadership. Burns has been credited with moving leadership studies beyond the Great Man idea and also beyond the Transactional Leader era. Both were shown by him to be inadequate to describe the effective leader. In their place he posits the idea of transformational leadership, which, at the outset, appears to place the values of the leader at the apex of the theory. "Leadership is not a neutral, mechanistic process," he writes, "but the transforming human moral factor in converting values into outcomes."[13]

These values are shared between the leaders and the people they lead. The clarification and articulation of these values and the action taken in light of these values are the basis of transformational leadership. Burns writes, "Transforming leaders define public values that embrace the supreme and enduring principles of people. Transforming values lie at the heart of transforming leadership, determining whether leadership indeed can be transforming."[14]

The problem in this view is not so much with the emphasis on values, but in the presupposition of what those values are.

> The pursuit of happiness must be our touchstone. . . . It encompasses the highest potentialities for transformation both in people's situations and in themselves. And it epitomizes, as perhaps no other phrase, what it is that many in this work—the millions and billions—most profoundly lack; the opportunity to shape and direct the quality and meaning of their own lives.[15]

By speaking of "the pursuit of happiness" Burns is making the philosophical point that all humanity is driven by a basic desire for happiness. By tapping into that common drive and giving it a voice and a vision, the leader can be effective in bringing about transformative change. Burns understands this is a process, but the end result is clear: "The ultimate attainment of happiness is a cherished dream, but as a goal of transforming leadership we must view it more as a process, a pursuit."[16]

Here we see the great divide between Burns's (and Thomas Jefferson's) understanding of the pursuit of happiness and the biblical call to the pursuit of faithfulness. The key is whether the human condition is basically good or sinful. If it is good, we can know what truly makes us happy, and we can pursue that happiness in ways that do not cost our neighbor his or her happiness.

If human nature is basically sinful apart from redemption in Christ, the pursuit of happiness is a self-serving quest that will bring only bondage to self-preservation at all costs. Even the concept of service devolves into a search for personal meaning in which relationships become means and not ends. The best we can hope for is a mutual pursuit of self-interests that don't come into conflict. In contrast, in the kingdom of God, relationships can only be ends, not means.

Burns's Enlightenment values are based on a utopian idea that we both know and can pursue those things that bring us happiness and that there is a value system common to all people that allows us to undertake that pursuit without harming our neighbor. Christian doctrine and the daily testimony of the world around us render this utopian idea baseless.

Leadership and the new science. Wheatley's contribution to leadership studies moved us away from "the old story" of dominion, control and all-encompassing materialism. This old story saw all of life as basically mechanistic and therefore within our grasp to dissect, evaluate, understand and ultimately control, although usually without success. "Since nothing is as controllable as we hope," she writes, "we soon become entangled in a cycle of exerting control, failing to control, exerting harsher control, failing again, panicking."[17]

This is a contribution worth celebrating. Wheatley's conception of an organization as a living, breathing organism is far closer to the biblical understanding of the community of God than Transactional Leadership theory's mechanistic view of the universe. Wheatley seems to come near to the steward leader idea when she talks about the dynamic quality of leadership, the role of freedom and our reliance on imperatives that define both life and community.

The problem comes when she defines what, for her, are the two great imperatives for leadership. For the first she uses a biological definition of life: "Life's first imperative is that it must have the freedom to create itself. Life begins with this primal freedom to create, the capacity for self-determination."[18] Wheatley describes this as the freedom to decide what to notice, what to invest with meaning. It is free to decide what its reaction will be, whether it will change or not.

If we were perfectly good, this might have some promise. But if we need a radical transformation that sets us free from a fallen human nature, this strategy will actually lead not to freedom but to bondage.

We will be free only to replicate who we already are. Without real transformation, but only with self-transformation, Wheatley has thrown us back on ourselves yet again, having to find everything we need within our own supposed autonomous inherent goodness.

We have another glimmer of hope, however, when she speaks of life as "system-seeking," looking for community and connectedness.[19] This might remind us that we are created in the image of a triune God for relationship and mutual interdependence. But it is, according to Wheatley, through the evolutionary process that the individual will always move to the communal.

The problem, as Wheatley sees it, is that communities and institutions "lack clarity about why they are together."[20] The result is that communities and organizations "serve us only as mirrors that reflect back to us the lack of cohering agreements at the heart of our community."[21] The solution is to find the "organizing center or heart of the community." This, she claims, will come from conversation that connects us "in a deeper place."

Wheatley has reintroduced us to the reality that we were made for relationships, and she has given us a wonderful glimpse into the need for human connectedness and the fundamental value of community and creativity. She has served to move leadership and organizational studies away from the old story of "man as machine" and has provided a polemic against the life-destroying quality of the "control and dominate" approach to human activity, organizational life and leadership effectiveness. Unfortunately, her wholesale commitment to the secular humanist position of the basic, even if now conceived as corporate, goodness of the human spirit leaves her solutions in the clouds.

The problem for Wheatley remains her total reliance on corporate human goodness to connect ethically, to dialogue with integrity, to be able to see beyond our pursuit of happiness, to find reasons for the kind of selflessness and self-sacrifice required to connect at this deeper place. Yet there is no evidence that the corporate human spirit will continually and faithfully pursue these. Quite the opposite. If the center, the "deeper place," is not the transforming presence of Jesus Christ, and if the values are not kingdom values that free us to be selfless and self-giving, the reality of Wheatley's dream will always disappoint, and communities and organizations will continually entangle themselves in different sets of bondages. Her approach once again throws us back on our corporate selves to connect at this deeper place, when we were created for a distinctly different purpose.

Wheatley sums it up in a section titled "We can rely on human goodness."

> We *are* our only hope for creating a future worth working for. We can't go it alone, we can't get there without each other and we can't create it without relying anew on our fundamental and precious human goodness.[22]

> I believe in these dark times that we can rely only on the hope, resiliency and love that is found in the human spirit.[23]

If our only hope is the goodness found within us (individually or corporately), we are in deep trouble indeed! As Christians who are called to lead, we rely on only one hope, which is so eloquently described in the classic hymn "Rock of Ages":

> Should my tears forever flow, should my zeal no languor know,
> All for sin could not atone: thou must save and thou alone;
> In my hand no price I bring, simply to thy cross I cling.

Servant leadership. Of all the leadership theories of the past fifty years, none has been embraced as much by the Christian community as Servant Leadership. Greenleaf has opened up for us a view of leadership that comes as close to the values of the kingdom of God as any other in recent history. His passion for effective leaders and his understanding that such leaders are servants *first* and leaders second, fits well with our study of the steward leader. Even the terms *servant* and *steward* are reciprocal at some levels. Servant leadership challenges us to rethink leadership at the fundamental level of the motives and heart of the leader. Only those who have the "natural feeling that one wants to serve, to serve *first*"[24] are worthy of following. Greenleaf refers to this person as a "natural servant, the person who is servant first."[25] Later he refers to servant leaders as "able servants with potential to lead."[26]

While his formulation of the traits and activities of the servant leader is extremely helpful and serves to move leadership studies well ahead of the former approaches, in the end there is no explanation of why a person would ever be a servant in the first place. The concept of "natural servant" leads one to conclude that there is, again, some capacity in the human condition that tends toward servanthood as an innate characteristic. Even in Greenleaf's work in church leadership, he never defines the source of the capacity for servanthood but leaves open the view that it is somehow part of the basic goodness in humanity—a view that has proven to be the Achilles heel for other secular leadership theories.

The Steward Leader Model. From the Great Man theory through Strategic Leadership and beyond, the steward leader model stands apart in three ways: First, these theories start with acts of leadership deemed to be effective and try to work back to find common traits and characteristics. Second, they rely on the basic goodness of human nature as the basis for the work of leadership. And third, they have a common view that the leader moves people toward the goal of personal happiness with the hope and belief that people—and leaders—can actually know what makes them happy and can pursue it without harming their neighbor.

The steward leader approach is based on the transformation that takes place in the heart of the leader as a faithful and godly steward, and works from this inner transformation (which is ongoing) to the outward impact when a godly steward is called to lead. This inward-outward direction and the emphasis of being over doing set the steward leader apart from this array of secular leadership theories.

The steward leader model also takes seriously the Christian doctrine of original sin. The very term *steward* denotes dependence on the one who is the true owner. And that complete ownership calls for holistic stewardship. Again, our self-understanding is based on the person and work of Jesus Christ. That is, in the mirror we see a person created for wholeness, a person lost through sin and a person redeemed in Christ. This kingdom view gives us both our absolute dependence on God and our utter and complete freedom in that dependence. Without the atoning work of Jesus Christ we have no basis for hope. Rather than searching for some hidden inner goodness, we rely wholly on the supreme goodness of our Creator God and his promise to work in us and through us for our transformation into his image. That is a radically different understanding of human nature, and it distinguishes the steward leader approach from the secular models discussed.

Finally, the steward leader takes seriously our utter incapacity both to know what makes us happy and to be able to pursue that happiness without negatively impacting our neighbor's pursuit of the same. Even further, it rejects the notion that our purpose in life is to pursue our own happiness, replacing it with the values of the kingdom of God, which entreat us to pursue joyful obedience in our calling as godly and therefore holistic stewards.

Faith-Based Leadership Studies

Over the past thirty years there has been a proliferation of writing and teaching on leadership from a faith-based perspective. Writers such as Peter Drucker, Warren Bennis, Max De Pree and Ted Engstrom have contributed immeasurable value to the field of leadership studies (see appendix one). More recently, leaders like Bill Hybels, Leonard Sweet, John MacArthur and Bill Robinson have added to this immense corpus of writing.

It is well beyond the scope of this chapter to compare and contrast the concept of the steward leader with this vast landscape of faith-based work on leadership. Instead, I will attempt a brief listing of five distinctions between the steward leader and the leadership types presented in these various works.

Docking the "ship." As I said at the outset, this is a "who" book not a "how" book. That alone distinguishes it from many faith-based approaches to leadership. I am surprised at the number of authors who see personal transformation as an add-on rather than as the primary distinction of a godly leader. In some works it is not brought up until nearly the end of the book and not treated in any integrated way with what has come before. In other works, even when it is incorporated as being of fundamental value to the effectiveness of a leader, it is often described as the transformation of the leader as a leader, not as a child of God who is then called to lead. I believe this is an important distinction. God's work of transforming our lives does not begin when we answer a call to lead. Transformation is also not confined to our role as leader, nor does it end when we leave a leadership position.

Our transformation into the likeness of Christ is the central, all-encompassing reality of our lives from the moment Christ enters our hearts until he takes us home. From time to time we may receive a vocational call to leadership, and ongoing transformation shapes and forms us uniquely for that work. However, that process remains larger than the work. We are transformed as spouses, parents, church members and neighbors all the while that we are also transformed as leaders. When leadership books focus only on the latter, they do not give us as rich a picture of the godly leader as we need.

Many other well-intentioned books are completely "doing-driven." They tend to communicate that godly leadership has nothing to do with a changed heart and everything to do with building teams, casting vision, empowering staff, raising money and discovering our leadership style. Most provide long to-do lists for us to accomplish. Checklists, traits and styles abound as we navigate our way through to find the real leader inside us. This outside-in movement is in sharp distinction to the development of a steward leader.

I have attempted to stay away from the terms leader*ship* and steward*ship*. As soon as we add the *ship*, we shift our focus from the "who" to the "how" and "what." It is my contention that in this rapidly changing world, the Holy Spirit is our sole guide to the particular way we work out our call to lead as a faithful steward. For that reason I have purposely "docked the *ship*" to ensure that we remain focused on this great work of being transformed into faithful stewards on all four levels, and the high calling of the steward leader.

Starting point. Another distinction lies in our respective starting points. It seems intuitive to start a discussion of effective leadership by examining what it looks like and working our way back from there to a set of common characteristics and traits of those who model it. If we can define effectiveness, if we know it when we see it, it seems plausible to trace the effect back to the cause. Then we examine the cause and see how we can re-create it in ourselves and others, presuming that when we do, we will engender the same effect.

This requires us to decide what works, and herein lies much of the debate in leadership studies. How do we define effectiveness in a ministry setting or even in a for-profit, secular setting? Do we measure effectiveness in bottom-line dollars, in strategic goals met, in employee morale, in mission accomplishment, in client satisfaction surveys? Do churches measure effectiveness by membership growth, program breadth, financial stability, building expansion, staff size or community engagement?

I have spent the past nine years as a consultant to faith-based, not-for-profit organizations and churches doing strategic planning. This question continues to challenge every client: how do you measure success? If you cannot measure success, you cannot delineate effective leadership. Even worse, if you identify the wrong markers of success, you will develop a flawed profile of the successful leader.

I believe that the common denominator in the life of every effective leader must be the commitment to be a godly steward. There is no research to examine whether such a commitment has historically led to effective leadership. I don't believe such research is either possible or necessary. We do not seek to be godly stewards *in order that* we may be effective leaders. This is not a cause-and-effect strategy; it is an act of obedience.

The call to be a godly steward is unequivocal for the Christian. It is not a technique that we decide to learn in order to lead well. There is no causal link with well-run organizations, happy employees or financial stability. Even if there were, it would not—*must not*—be the motivator for one to seek to be a godly steward. The order and motivation for this work is of supreme importance. If readers of this book respond by saying, "Well, we want to be effective leaders, so we had better learn what it means to be godly stewards," then they have missed the point. The only proper response is a humble admission of our need to set aside our penchant for ownership and come under the guidance of the Holy Spirit in the transformation of our hearts.

As this happens we may also be summoned to lead. If we are, we will take it on with a previously unknown sense of freedom, responding with joyful obedience. The result will likely be effectiveness for the kingdom of God, but not in a way that can allow the process to be traced. The work of the Holy Spirit in the life of a godly steward who is called to lead is simply too diverse, too varied and too rich to be categorized or reduced to a method or process.

From steps to trajectories. Sunday school teachers and CEOs of major ministries are leaders. Megachurch pastors and volunteer coordinators of small ministries are leaders. Congresswomen and den mothers, parents and presidents, school teachers and grandparents are leaders. Imagine trying to write the definitive "Ten Steps to Becoming an Effective Steward Leader" that covered every vocation in every setting with every people group pursuing every mission in every country? If we cannot arrive at a standard set of traits of an effective leader, we certainly cannot establish the steps such a leader must take to lead effectively.

This is not a cause for sorrow but for celebration. Moses did not lead like David or Esther or Nehemiah. Yet they all served God faithfully and effectively. They stood in their time with their skills, and the Holy Spirit worked through them to accomplish what God intended. The same is true for you and me. God starts with our hearts, and from there he works through us to achieve his good purposes. You don't have to worry that you have only six of the ten traits of a steward leader. God wants your heart, and the rest is up to how the Spirit chooses to work within you.

So I start with the heart of the godly steward. However, I do not want to set aside all discussion of what it might look like when godly stewards lead. Therefore, I will carefully present what I will call "trajectories." I will posit some ways in which steward leaders might serve their people and lead their organizations. The term *trajectory* indicates that we can only know the general direction this leadership might take, and we make a guess at its final destination. But I will not be formulaic or fall back into developing methodologies. I hope to keep the discussion at the level of trajectory, understanding that the Holy Spirit will always take us in directions that we could never have guessed or planned.

From calling to freedom. I agree with most faith-based authors that godly leaders are called or summoned to their vocation. Yet calling alone is not enough. Many faith-based works on leadership seem to imply that once a person is called, he or she is also equipped for effective leadership. It is an awesome thing to be called by God to serve in his kingdom. And we do not need to add anything to that calling for it to be genuine. Yet calling denotes a moment, while transformation describes an ongoing process that involves our whole life. And it is this transformation, not just the calling, that equips the steward for effective leadership.

I have attempted to ground this study in this work of transformation. I believe that transformation develops in us the heart of the godly steward. The product of that development is a heart set free to respond with a life of joyful obedience. Steward leaders are not effective because they are called, but because they are free. And in that freedom they render joyful obedience to serve as the person God created them to be.

Too many faith-based leadership studies miss this vital step. They move from the calling of a leader to the work of a leader without considering the preparation of the heart of a leader. They assume that if one is called, he or she is prepared, and so the discussion immediately shifts to the lists of works that exemplify good leaders.

The church of Jesus Christ is overwhelmed with men and women in leadership positions who have been called but who remain in bondage to an ownership approach. As owners they are either burning out or making serious ethical compromises. Earlier, in discussing my own journey, I considered the difference between being appointed and being anointed. Pastors are called and appointed. Ministry leaders respond to search committees and are hired. CEOs complete rigorous induction processes and are placed in positions of great authority. Yet in none of these processes do we often hear about how one confirms one's anointing.

A person's calling to a position of leadership and his anointing for that work are two separate acts. The anointing of the Holy Spirit for the job of leadership is a biblical imperative that we must raise up and understand in our recruitment of leaders. We must stop believing that calling is enough and take the responsibility to help leaders discover the freedom of the godly steward. Only from there can they become steward leaders who lead others freely and respond to every challenge with a heart of joyful obedience.

From model to Lord. In making this final distinction, I will likely anger some of my colleagues. But hear me out. I do not believe that Jesus came to show us how to be good leaders. I do not believe that he set himself up as a model for effective leadership or that he calls us to fashion our leadership style according to the way he lived and served while on this earth.

I could even make the point that if we believe there are traits of effective leadership, as many have set them out, then Jesus was a very ineffective leader. How would you rate a leader if you were given the following information about his work: he chose ill-prepared people who did not understand his mission; he so frequently spoke in veiled and unclear language that the people he came to lead seldom understood what he was saying, and most left him in frustration; he concealed his true mission from even his closest associates until the very end of his term; he angered those in authority who could have been an asset to his work; he made such outrageous claims about his abilities that all but a handful of followers turned against him; one of his own team members testified against him to the police; his closest friend denied he ever knew him; when he left for a time, his team was in total disarray and completely demoralized; and it was left to those who followed him to reassemble the team, recruit new members and build an organization. How excited would you be to lift this person up as your model for leadership?

Jesus came not to provide us a role model but to proclaim the coming of the kingdom of God; to preach good news to the poor, release to the captives, to restore sight to the blind and proclaim the year of the Lord's favor (see Luke 4:18-19). He came to be a sacrifice for the sins of all humanity, to rise triumphantly and to send his people out into the world to proclaim the message of hope and salvation. He completed in his life, death and resurrection everything we could not do, and now we are called to participate in that completed work as faithful and obedient followers. My point is that Jesus came to be the Lord of our life, not our example of good leadership.[27]

I do not deny that many of the traits lifted up as exemplifying effective leaders can be found in the life of Jesus. What I caution against is seeing in Jesus a model for right behavior instead of seeing the author and finisher of our faith. Jesus did not come to show us how to live so we might adjust our behavior to be more like him; he came to give us new life that is radically different from anything we know.

So our response is not to try to "be like Jesus," as if by changing some attitudes and tweaking some behaviors we suddenly can emulate the King of kings and Lord of lords. Our response is to deny ourselves, take up our cross and follow him. If we seek to save our life through a process of adjusting our attitudes to be more Christlike, we will lose it. It is only in losing this life completely for the sake of Christ that we will find our true life. That transformation is at the heart of the godly steward, and it is substantially different from a call to change our behavior in order to be a leader like Jesus.[28]

The steward leader has been set free to live a life of joyful obedience in all he or she does. We need no model in order to do this. Jesus Christ is our one true Lord, and in the power of the Holy Spirit he lives in the leader and guides him or her day by day. Far from being a past example from history, Jesus is a living, dynamic presence in the daily life of the steward leader. Author Steve Korch reminds us, "It is not a self-reformed life that is impressive to those around us; it is a God-transformed life that demands explanation."[29]

This study of the steward leader draws from and builds on many of the great works that have gone before, from both faith-based and secular writers and scholars. These five areas distinguish this call to be a steward leader from much of what has been written on the subject from a faith-based perspective.

PART THREE

FOUR TRANSFORMATIONS AND FOUR TRAJECTORIES

I HAVE ESTABLISHED SOME HARD AND FAST RULES for the way we talk about the steward leader. I must be careful here in part three not to regress back into talk about traits, characteristics or tactics. Yet I must also not ignore the fact that steward leaders are called to lead effectively, and that effectiveness is tangible and real. I also affirm that there are some experiences shared by effective steward leaders from which we can learn. It is acceptable within this framework to "see how it works" as long as we use these glimpses as motivation and not as methodology.

For that reason I want to share the four transformations of every steward leader. Each work of transformation is unique, and together they are the process whereby the Holy Spirit forms and shapes godly stewards into steward leaders. At each level of this work I will offer both a *gift* that is ours in this transformation and a *temptation* that will pull at the heart of every steward leader. I will conclude with a *spiritual discipline* that can serve us as we undergo this dynamic work of the Spirit and prepare ourselves to be more faithful, obedient steward leaders.

From each of these transformations I will then propose *trajectories* that our work must take as we live out our transformation as godly stewards in our lives as steward leaders. These trajectories will focus on the impact each transformation will have on the *people* we serve and, through them, the *organizations* we lead. In each of these discussions I will be careful not to slide back into language of techniques or steps in a process. This is as much the Holy Spirit's work as it is our inner transformation. I will look instead at where each may lead us if we are true to our calling as steward leaders. I will not describe the target, for that would align us with the leadership theories with which I have drawn such a sharp distinction. I will, however, talk about the movement to which we are called, and we will listen to voices of Christian leaders who are on that trajectory.

Below is a matrix of these transformations and trajectories. It is laid out on two axes: spheres of transformation and levels of relationship. Each column heading identifies one of three spheres of transformation in the steward leader's life and work: transformation in the life of the steward, in the lives of people the steward leads and in the organization the steward serves. The rows direct us to each of the four levels of relationship that we are called to steward: with God, with ourselves, with others and with God's creation. The spheres of transformation intersect with the four levels of relationship. By moving across the rows we can see the trajectory of how our call to steward each level of relationship affects all three spheres of transformation. We will look at these trajectories by moving across each of the four rows.

By definition, you as a steward leader are on a journey of transformation. My goal is to describe as best I can the trajectories involved in that journey. How this journey unfolds, where it ultimately leads, and what is learned and produced along the way is your story. It is unique to you, your people and your organization. It is God's work in you and through you, and you are only the steward of this journey. Therefore, your sole responsibility is joyful and obedient response to that provision and calling and anointing. May that be the source of your humble attitude, your hope and your freedom for the work to which you are called.

Table 1. The Steward Leader Matrix

4 LEVELS	TRANSFORMATION in the Life of the Steward Leader	TRAJECTORIES	
		In the Life of the People He/She Leads	In the Life of the Organization He/She Leads
LEVEL One Transformation	The Steward Leader in the Presence of God	Steward Leaders Are United with the People They Serve	Steward Leaders Cultivate Culture
Stewards of Our Relationship with God, Our Creator	Having been recipients of God's love and mercy we respond to the Spirit's work of transforming grace in us by stewarding our relationship with God through personal devotion, corporate worship, prayer and the commitment to grow as his disciples.	We lead others in ways that reflect our priority of engendering in our people hearts that are rich toward God, enabling them to attain to the fullest expression of their God-given talents and to live out to the fullest their unique vocation as members of his kingdom.	We create corporate culture that values the priority of this relationship in all employees and that supports, encourages and empowers them to respond to this stewardship call through their roles in our organizations in pursuit of the highest standards of excellence.
LEVEL Two Transformation	The Steward Leader in the Mirror	Steward Leaders Develop Whole People	Steward Leaders Harness the Power of People
Stewards of Our Relationship with Our Self, as Children of God, Our Creator	Having been redeemed by God in Christ as his beloved child, we respond by stewarding our self-image, that it may reflect both our natural state as sinners in need of grace and our status as forgiven and beloved children of God and heirs to the kingdom.	We lead others in ways that recognize the ongoing work of the Spirit in their lives, shaping and forming them into the people of God they were created to be, and encouraging them in finding the balance in their lives that will enable them to be effective workers in the kingdom of God.	We set policy, develop employees, invest resources and set expectations that combine accountability and rewards in ways that build employee morale, personal growth, team work and innovation for greater organizational effectiveness and employee satisfaction and retention.
LEVEL Three Transformation	The Steward Leader in Relationship	Steward Leaders Build and Value Community as Its Own End	Steward Leaders Are Caretakers of Their Community
Stewards of Our Relationships with Our Neighbors	Having been given back our status before God, we respond by stewarding our relationships with others by humbly serving our neighbor, valuing our relationships as ends and not means, embracing sacrifice and the ministry of presence, and glorying in the triumphs of others.	We lead others in ways that value true community, we understand and invest in best practices that build and strengthen interpersonal relationships, we set goals and measure results according to relational standards, and we encourage sacrifice in the pursuit of individual and organizational growth.	We build business plans and create stategies that capitalize on our focus on relationships as the operating paradigm for everything we do, recognizing the power of serving one another and valuing relationships as the basis of organizational health and effectiveness.
LEVEL Four Transformation	The Steward Leader in God's Creation	Steward Leaders Marshal Resources Effectively	Steward Leaders Create Organizational Consistency and Witness
Stewards of Our Relationship with God's Creation	Having been restored to our place as caretakers of God's good creation, we respond by stewarding our resources of time, talent and treasure in ways that care for our environment, demonstrate our freedom from materialism and bear witness to our vocation as God's faithful stewards.	We lead others in ways that encourage and challenge them to live as stewards of God's abundant supply through their roles as coworkers, leaders and innovators, equipping them to use effectively all of the resources God has made available to them and through them for his glory.	We cast vision, plan strategy and set goals that direct our organization in ways that reflect our commitment to be holistic stewards as a community, resulting in greater organizational effectiveness, missional consistency and a clearer witness of our calling to care for God's creation.

4

STEWARDS OF OUR RELATIONSHIP
WITH OUR CREATOR GOD

LEVEL ONE TRANSFORMATION

| The Steward in the Presence of God | Steward Leaders Are United with the People They Serve | Steward Leaders Cultivate Culture |

THE STEWARD LEADER IN THE PRESENCE OF GOD

When godly stewards are called to lead, they must seek to find that place where their work as stewards of their relationship to God intersects their call to lead. What they find is that this relationship comes under attack almost from the moment they assume their leadership role. The enemy works his deceptive ways in all of us, but Christian leaders are especially set up for the worst the enemy has to bring. The reason is easy to see: when leaders fall, they take so much of the kingdom with them. They take the reputations of their ministry or church; they take the trust of their people; they take the loyalty of their supporters; they take their witness in their community; and they take the confidence of other leaders or those who may someday be called to lead. Any believer who has ever taken on a leadership role knows exactly what I mean.

The first place where this attack will be felt is in the battle for your relationship with God. In light of this battle I believe that the steward leader is given the gift of an extraordinary sense of intimacy with God and faces an extraordinary temptation to let that relationship stagnate.

The Gift of Intimacy

The gift God has for us as stewards of our relationship with him is the precious gift of intimacy. Hebrews calls us to "approach the throne of grace with confidence" (Hebrews 4:16). To the Romans, Paul wrote, "For you did not receive a spirit that makes you a slave again to fear, but you received the Spirit of sonship. And by him we cry, *'Abba*, Father'" (Romans 8:15).

We steward this gift through the disciplines of worship, prayer, fasting, meditation on God's Word, devotion, simplicity, solitude, submission, service, confession and celebration.[1] As we practice each, we act as stewards of this gift of intimate relationship with our Creator. Richard Foster reminds us that "the Classic disciplines of the spiritual life call us to move beyond surface living into the depths."[2]

I was sitting on the beach during a family vacation in Belize, taking in the beauty of the Caribbean as it splashed its way onto the sandy shore. Children were playing along the shoreline, running to stay ahead of the waves as if chased by a ferocious beast. Some of it was play, but some was a real fear of the power of the incoming waves. Older kids had conquered that fear and were splashing in the waves, even riding the occasional small one onto the shore. They stayed in water that was still shallow, but they were out in the waves. Still older kids and some adults had paddled out beyond the first sets of waves and were swimming in deeper water, riding larger waves and having the time of their lives. As I looked further out, I could see groups of snorkelers, heads down, occasional spurts of water shooting from their snorkels. Once in a while, one would stick his head up and shout to his comrades about the beauty of the fish.

Meanwhile, just leaving the dock was a boat filled with scuba divers heading out to the famous Blue Hole. A brochure on the various dives had told me that novices could go out and do dives of thirty to fifty feet and see incredible fish and coral that the snorkelers would never see. The more experienced could dive further to where schools of rays and other wonders could be seen. Finally, the most experienced divers could use the oxygen-nitrogen mixture to dive well past one hundred feet into the Blue Hole and see wonders that few on the planet would ever witness.

As I considered this beautiful scene, it seemed that there was a powerful theological lesson to be learned here. (Why we theologians can't just sit on a beach without coming up with some theological analogy, I'll never know!) Everyone wants to go deeper. Occasionally, one of the youngest kids, coaxed by the older ones, would cautiously venture out to try to join those swimming in deeper water, only to scurry back to the safer place where she could always feel the sand under her feet.

Swimmers looked out to the snorkelers and wondered what amazing sights they were missing. Snorkelers watched the scuba divers motoring past, wishing they could join them on a dive. And I am sure that at the Blue Hole, while those at thirty feet were awestruck by the scenes swimming by in front of them, they couldn't help but wish that they could join the experienced divers who disappeared into the deep blue waters below.

So it should be in our life with God. Our transformation is a journey, and journeys are, by definition, movements. When you sit down, your journey is placed on hold. When you stop growing, your transformation stalls. When you ignore your guide and go your own way, your journey may turn into a nightmare. Jesus promised us, "When . . . the Spirit of truth comes, he will guide you into all truth" (John 16:13). As the Holy Spirit guides us into truth, along this journey of transformation, he always beckons us into deeper water.

Now, deeper water is almost always a scary place to journey. Deeper water means less control. Remember the first time you swam into the waves and suddenly couldn't feel the sand under your feet? Scary stuff! Deeper water challenges our faith in our guide. Have you ever tried to teach a young child to snorkel? It is completely unnatural to put your face in the water and breathe. I have seen parents almost screaming at their kids, "Just take a breath, for crying out loud!" For all their trust in their parents, it's just not right to them.

Yet the Spirit calls us, beckons us and gently leads us out into deeper water than we have ever experienced. He calls us to trust, to cling even more tightly to him, to put our face in the water *and breathe*. When we do, we also slowly open our eyes, and before us is a sight like we have never seen before. The rewards for going deeper are immeasurable, and God wants that for every one of us. He wants such a level of intimacy that we will walk out into deeper water with him.

The question for the steward leader is, what for you is the next deeper step? No matter where we are in our spiritual journey, no matter how seasoned, how spiritually mature, how biblically knowledgeable or how revered, there is for each of us a "next deeper step." Whatever it may be, it will require of us a new level of intimacy with our Savior. We can go deeper when we draw closer, hold tighter and trust more deeply in the one who calls us out beyond the waves.

Leaders who remain content to splash along in the ankle-deep waves are heading for trouble. And leaders who venture out into deeper water without their guide will surely drown. Where are you?

This image of the call to deeper water demonstrates again the magnificent gift of freedom that is ours in Christ. Intimacy with God requires a freedom of spirit that comes only as a gift from God. He not only has saved us, but also has equipped us to respond to him with an open heart, free to love and trust and obey. Our transformation is a journey to freedom.

As we are freed, we are able through God's power to journey to depths beyond our wildest dreams. Paul describes Christ as the one "who is able to do immeasurably more than all we ask or imagine, according to his power that is at work within us" (Ephesians 3:20).

Christ wants to do in you immeasurably more than you could even imagine. That means richer intimacy, greater freedom and deeper water. There is a question that is logical to ask about this deeper water: "Is it safe out there?" After all, there are sharks out there, and stinging jellyfish and strong currents. If we are to go plunging into the deeper waters into which God is calling us, can we be sure the journey will be safe? The answer is an unequivocal no! Jesus does not promise us safety. In fact he warns us that going deeper will cost us everything: "If anyone would come after me, he must deny himself and take up his cross daily and follow me. For whoever wants to save his life will lose it, but whoever loses his life for me will save it" (Luke 9:23-24). Going deeper means living even more completely the values of the kingdom of God, which place us in direct conflict with the values of this world. Going deeper means loving more, sacrificing more and standing even more firmly as our faith requires. All of these are not safe places to live, not at all.

Perhaps the most accurate words spoken on this subject came from the mouth of a beaver. In C. S. Lewis's *The Lion, the Witch and the Wardrobe*, Lucy Pevensie is learning about Aslan, the great lion who rules Narnia. In hearing him described by Mr. Beaver as a King of the Beasts and the Great Lion, and that anyone approaching him will have her knees knocking, Lucy replies, "Then he isn't safe?" And Mr. Beaver replies incredulously, "Safe? Who said anything about safe? Course he isn't safe. But He is good. He is the King, I tell you."[3]

The one who stands in deeper water and calls us to come to him does not promise us a calm and safe journey, *but he is good, he is the King!* And for that reason, we come.

In our journey of transformation we are daily being freed for this work. It is only in freedom that we grow, that we journey out to the Blue Hole and prepare for the deep dives of life. When we set aside our penchant for control, even in our relationship to God, we are set free to wade out beyond our comfort level.

Intimacy is the foundation for this freedom. Do not let this gift become a burden or a duty. It is in our freedom that we joyfully respond to God's call to deeper intimacy. Our devotional time, our prayer life, our worship and our meditation on God's Word are free and joyous responses. And they are the foundation on which every steward leader must stand.

The Temptation of Stagnancy

If intimacy is the gift at this first level, then stagnancy is the temptation. Ironically, it is our doing nature that breeds rather than overcomes this stagnancy. For the godly steward, the call to lead must be simultaneously a call to greater depth in our relationship with God. Yet so often the opposite occurs. As the demands of the job pile up, our time and focus on this life-giving relationship diminish. Our people expect us to be both physically present everywhere and spiritually prepared at all times. No leader can do both, and too often we trade the quiet time of spiritual preparation for physical presence at meetings, events, fundraisers and the like.

We must see this trade-off as a deal with the devil. It is nothing less than a capitulation to depending a little more on our own strength and a little less on God's; trusting a little more in our own ideas and a little less on God's wisdom; being a little more content with listening to our own voice and those of our people than to the "still, small voice" of the Holy Spirit.

There are three symptoms of this stagnancy: self-reliance, distance and shallowness.

Self-reliance. Self-reliance is the subtle dethroning of God from the center of our lives. In the life of the leader under siege this does not happen overtly, but subtly. The enemy does not storm in and demand that we deny Christ and take the throne of our lives by force. Instead, it happens in little ways, edging its way into our lives. It is the result of a slow loss of daily intimacy with God.

One beautiful autumn day in my Seattle-area home, I had a load of wood delivered for our wood stove. Instead of paying extra for the wood to be split, I bought it in rounds, thinking I would save money and get some exercise in the process. The truck dumped a large load of rounds in my yard, averaging about twenty-four inches across. As it pulled away, I was impressed by the size of the pile and the amount of work that awaited me.

So, in typical macho, lumberjack fashion I donned my best leather gloves, grasped the handle of my heavy splitting maul and positioned the first hunk of wood directly in front of me. I set my feet firmly, squared my shoulders, eyed the center of that piece of wood, drew back the mighty maul and with a powerful swing brought the full force of its sharp edge slamming perfectly into the dead center of the round.

The sound it made was not what I expected. Instead of the crack of wood splitting, the blow I delivered reverberated with a quiet "thuptt." The maul's edge bounced off as if repelled by some demon force, and the round glared back at me, unphased. I smiled confidently and thought, *Must be a knot.* So I repositioned the round and repeated the process, only again to hear the benign "thuptt." A bead of sweat trickled down my forehead as I weighed my options.

Clearly force was my only weapon, so I began furiously flailing at the piece of wood, which didn't seem to mind much. It just sat there, enduring my blows as my calm demeanor turned to frustration and then outright panic as I considered the pile of fifty or so recalcitrant rounds of wood waiting for me. Finally, with my knees shaking, my arms quivering from the repeated swings of the heavy maul and sweat blurring my vision, I took one last desperate swing. I missed my mark, significantly. Instead of hitting the center, I nearly missed the entire log. My maul caught the round only about two inches in from the edge. And an incredible thing happened. Crack! A piece of the formerly unconquerable log came flying off. As I stopped to study the situation for a moment, it dawned on me that I didn't need to (and couldn't, for that matter) split the log down the middle. Instead of one fatal blow to the center, the log was hewn by a succession of lighter blows around the edges.

One by one, each swing brought the cracking sound and pieces separating from the main log. Within just a few moments, with less work and only a few well-placed strokes, the one invincible round lay in ten pieces around me. What was left was the center piece, still bearing the marks of multiple blows to which it had not yielded. However, this time I took one easy swing, hit the same marks I had created in vain earlier, and the log, no longer surrounded by the mass of wood that had been chipped away, split straight down the middle and fell in pieces at my feet.

I learned a great lesson that day, far beyond how to split logs. The enemy seldom attacks us with blows to the center of our faith. He knows there is too much strength to destroy us with such a frontal attack. So instead he plans his blows more carefully and lands them more strategically. Quietly, without much fuss, he works away at us around the edges. There he finds it much easier to split off little pieces that go almost unnoticed.

These pieces are the small compromises we make in our time with our Lord. They are the little, seemingly harmless concessions we make to self-reliance. They are the growing number of times we work in our own strength and according to our own wisdom. They are the trade-offs we make to be more visible and active in our leadership roles. Slowly, piece by piece, compromise by compromise, we are being hewn like wood. And the cost is our intimacy with God.

We overcome self-reliance with submission, not with more doing. The key for us here is that stagnancy is a symptom of our *doing*, not our lack of doing. The more we seek to do, the more we fail to be. Author and pastor Douglas Webster writes, "Taking initiative is not the starting point for spiritual growth. . . . Instead of a quest for success there needs to be a rest for the soul, from which life's meaning, purpose and significance issue."[4]

We see that even here we must identify and avoid the temptation of a doing-dominated way of life. For it is easy to insert ourselves as the primary actor in this process. By doing so, we destroy the very thing we are seeking to attain. Hannah Whitehall Smith puts it this way:

> Man's part is to trust, God's part is to work. . . . Plainly the believer can do nothing but trust; while the Lord in whom he trusts, actually does the work entrusted to Him. . . . Your part is simply to rest. His part is to sustain you; and He cannot fail.[5]

Distance. Steve Korch describes the sense of distance from God as a symptom of the stagnancy that comes when we value our work over our character. Oswald Sanders looks at it from another angle, noting that when we ignore our stewardship of our relationship with God, it is we who have created the distance we feel: "Both Scripture and experience teach us that it is we, not God, who determine the degree of intimacy with Him that we enjoy. We are at this moment as close to God as we really choose to be."[6]

When we fail to submit ourselves wholly to God, we commit ourselves to an unauthentic spiritual life. We may still go through the motions, but we end up dishonest with God and impersonating life. The result is a sense of distance from God, and the fruit is disappointment with God.[7]

To overcome this distance we must recapture intimacy with our loving God. Again we find that it is in our "being" that we find intimacy with God. The surrender of the will is an essential element of that intimacy. In it we acknowledge our weakness and place ourselves under the authority of God's Word. Korch writes of God's longing for us:

> I long to draw you close and bless you with the warmth of my presence. Time alone will not provide this. If you do not capture my presence in the eternity of each moment, time will simply become the space that defines your boredom. I have not intended for you to live a sedentary spirituality.[8]

Draw near to God, and he will draw near to you.

Shallowness. When we cling to the shallows and refuse the call to go deeper into unknown waters, we face stagnation. We were not created for the shallows. God has so much more for us out in the deeper water. It is fear that causes us to shrink back from the plunge, and pride that provides the false sensation that "I can do everything I need to from the shoreline, thank you very much!"

One of the most terrifying places to find yourself is working in a leadership position vocationally while you are still splashing around in the shallow waves spiritually. This is the place from which leaders begin to hoard power and make ethical compromises. Shallow leaders are easy prey for the sexual and financial temptations that always lurk around the power that comes with leadership. With their journey of transformation on hold and intimacy with God receding, these leaders are left fully exposed to the attacks of the enemy.

We must move from spiritual shallowness to the next deeper step in our relationship with God. "If we don't move deeper into the Christian life, we are doomed to fight border skirmishes the rest of our life," Korch says.[9] Until we go deeper, we are left to fight with our old nature, constantly gazing back into the former life and fighting battles with it over and over again.

Self-reliance, distance and shallowness are the great enemies of our intimacy with God. They lead to stagnancy and leave us standing on the shore. As stewards of our relationship with God, we must recognize these danger signs. When we are called to be steward leaders, the danger signs must become blaring horns.

The great news is that the God who created us, saved us and now daily awaits our response to his gentle calling into deeper waters is a long-suffering and patient God. He will not drag us into the surf kicking and screaming. Neither will he give up on us and leave us to ourselves. He will always call, always offer, always wait.

What is the next deeper step in your relationship with God?

A Discipline: Praying for a Restoration of a Thirst for Intimacy

Every day in the life of a steward leader must begin with a thirst for intimacy with God. Pray for it, cultivate it, repent of the obstacles you have placed in front of it, expect it as a gift from God, and celebrate it when it is found. This thirst is a gift, but it must be sought and received.

Start your day with a prayer that asks God to restore in you the thirst and hunger for deeper intimacy with him. David prayed, "Restore to me the joy of your salvation" (Psalm 51:12). That daily prayer of restoration is the discipline of the steward leader. As God answers this sincere prayer, the habits and practices you will need to maintain this intimacy—and to go deeper with Christ—will be revealed through your time with God. There is no formula for greater intimacy, just a heart that yearns for it daily.

LEVEL ONE TRAJECTORIES

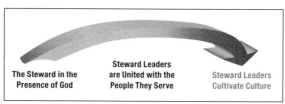

The Steward in the Presence of God | Steward Leaders are United with the People They Serve | Steward Leaders Cultivate Culture

STEWARD LEADERS ARE UNITED WITH THE PEOPLE THEY SERVE

In this trajectory I ask the question, "How would steward leaders serve their people at this first level?" Everything I have said about the steward leader in the presence of God leads me to this one conclusion: steward leaders are free to be united with the people they serve in a mutual journey of faith and discovery.

As we undergo the transformation of our own heart in our response to the call to be a godly steward, we become leaders who are passionate about the hearts of our people. We create new ways of setting priorities for leadership that impact the goals for our people and, through them, our organization. As a result, our people are enabled to attain the richest expression of their God-given talents and empowered to live to the fullest their unique vocation.

As steward leaders we can do this only because we ourselves have been set free. In this freedom, we can look beyond our personal needs and genuinely care about the spiritual well-being of our people. When I have real intimacy with God, I also have a huge capacity to want the same for the people I lead. If I live in the shallows, I have neither the security in my relationship with God nor the spiritual maturity to provide genuine spiritual leadership to my people.

What I end up doing is competing at precisely the place where I should be enabling and encouraging growth and discovery. My competition requires me to grasp at the trappings of spirituality to hide my deficiencies. I need to look like I am deep-sea diving when I cannot even operate a snorkel. Too many leaders are operating in the spiritual shallows, and they are acting out a charade publicly while privately competing with the people they are called to serve.

Steward leaders invite their people to join them in deeper waters. They yearn for every colleague to take his or her own next deeper step in relationship with Christ. And they are not threatened when they look out and find a coworker who has ventured even further than they. In fact, they are free to rejoice. This is real freedom, to have confidence in the depths into which God has called you, to winsomely urge others to go deeper with you and to rejoice when some find even deeper waters than your own.

However, it is not enough simply to desire this growth for your people. The steward leader must assemble the systems and shape the culture that will encourage and support such a process. You cannot say you are committed to a mutual journey of faith and discovery if your systems penalize people for time committed to spiritual disciplines and your culture rewards only doing-driven behavior. Systems and culture will ultimately prevail, and so they must be changed to support the goals of the steward leader.

It might rightly be asked what impact such changes might have on the measurable outcomes and financial bottom line of a ministry, church or business. Is this steward leader approach just wishful thinking that falls apart in the "real world"? Let me offer two responses. First, steward leaders have only one calling: obedient response to the call of God. If that response is to care about and be committed to the well-being of the people they lead, they will trust God for the outcomes. For the owner-leader, such a thought is impossible to imagine. Tied to the outward success of the organization, owner-leaders default to the most expedient way to achieve their definition of success. If people grow along the way, that is serendipitous. The owner-leader has tied his or her success to that of the organization and is in bondage to that success. For this leader, it would be unthinkable to risk the outward accomplishment of the organization for some less tangible goal like the spiritual growth of its people. The steward leader, however, seeks only to be obedient to Christ, which always puts him or her in a kingdom mindset. When we look at the world with a kingdom mindset, priorities shift dramatically, as does the definition of success.

This brings us to my second answer: the kingdom of God *is* the real world. Since when did following God's leading with absolute obedience come into conflict with the goals of a Christian organization? Yet, when steward leaders lift up the spiritual well-being of their people as a primary goal of the ministry, many raise the concern that such actions will divert attention from the mission of the organization—as if developing a community of men and women more deeply in love with Jesus would prove a bad investment of time for a ministry whose mission is to serve in Jesus' name!

Steward leaders must constantly hold a kingdom view, and they can do this because they enjoy intimacy with God. They must lead others according to this kingdom view, and they can do this because they are free.

| The Steward in the Presence of God | Steward Leaders are United with the People They Serve | Steward Leaders Cultivate Culture |

STEWARD LEADERS CULTIVATE CULTURE

When the participants in an organization undergo personal transformation in their relationship with God, a new culture emerges. The steward leader looks for, engenders, nourishes and protects this emerging culture as the foundation for the transformation of the business or ministry. This culture is a product of free people working together to glorify God. It is the antithesis of a culture of control in which people work to complete tasks like cogs in a wheel.

One result of this freedom is a constructive culture where people look first to work in teams rather than retreat to silos. They create an atmosphere where team members wrestle in discussions to discover productive solutions that are possible only when the best from each team member is synthesized into a solid decision. In such a culture there is no place for a watered-down consensus to keep everyone happy; rather, vigorous debate thrives in the "iron sharpens iron" environment (Proverbs 27:17).

Steward leaders recognize the strength of a positive culture and its impact on organizational effectiveness. They encourage their team to set challenging goals—bold goals that raise the bar and lead to significant performance improvements. Teams shaped by this culture become willing to shake up their comfort zones as they focus on results. Freedom begets freedom!

A culture can either inhibit productivity or maximize it.[10] If left to chance, cultures decline instead of improve. If a culture is to be transformed, the leader must set the pace. Steward leaders lift those around them by their direct interaction and management, but also and most importantly by their example. Bill Robinson describes what he calls "grace-filled" leadership and its impact on culture:

Grace-filled leadership releases not only warmth but also energy into an organizational culture. Energy dissipates in a climate of fear. Mistakes are too costly. As we think about organizational culture in our ministries and organizations, we need to ask ourselves what kind of culture we're creating.[11]

Such grace-filled leadership creates a culture of trust and confidence. Steward leaders offer grace, and as they do, they cultivate a culture of grace that returns to them.

> It is in offering grace that we discover one of the most reliable and powerful leadership principles: *you get what you give.* When we trust, we are trusted. When we doubt, we are doubted. When we give the benefit of the doubt, we receive the benefit of doubt. Grace circles back to bless the leader. Over time, being filled with grace fills others with grace.[12]

For a steward leader to build a sustainable organization that performs far beyond its capabilities, culture is the bed of white-hot embers that keeps the flames burning. Jesus created an environment in which his disciples could follow him and discover the heart of God the Father. There were no mandatory meetings, no demands for higher productivity or threats for bad behavior. Instead, Jesus answered questions with parables and had patience with, and full acceptance of, those who would eventually lead the building of God's church. Jesus created a culture where people could rise beyond their situation and enter into a journey with eternal value. He was grace-filled in his words and actions.

For owner-leaders who seek control, culture will always be a struggle. A strong, controlling personality may be able to shape culture initially, but it cannot be maintained by one person for long. Culture, by its very definition, involves a community. If a leader is threatened by the loss of control, the challenge of shaping culture will devour him or her. Only in the freedom of a steward leader can a community be set free to form a culture that serves the mission and glorifies the real owner. Steward leaders seek to help shape culture, but they have no need to control it. If, under the guidance of the Holy Spirit, culture is shaped in a different way than the steward leader may have desired, there is grace to accept the change and lead onward.

Culture is also both a reflection of personality and transcendent of it. This brings us back to the importance of our response of joyful obedience. Because leaders influence the culture of the organizations they lead, steward leaders seek to create a free and obedient culture that is a reflection of their own freedom in Christ and obedience to his calling. If we believe that somehow our organization's culture is not impacted by our own behavior and values, we are either irresponsible or naïve.

To help us think about the impact of the leader on culture, consider the concept of fractals, which Margaret Wheatley uses to help us understand organizational culture. Fractals are complex structures that originate in simplicity. One example is a fern, which appears to be a complex structure of countless shapes and patterns woven together to form its intricate and beautiful leaves. Yet the entire structure can be simplified to a basic four-line pattern that is simply repeated in various directions and sizes. Many highly complex structures in the natural world can be simplified in a similar way to a basic fractal pattern. Wheatley writes, "All fractal patterns are created as individuals exercise both freedom and responsibility to effuse simple rules. Complex structures emerge over time from simple elements and rules, and autonomous interactions."[13]

Just as the most complex physical structures are composed of simple fractals repeated within the confines of a basic set of rules, so are organizations. Culture is formed from repeated patterns of behavior. Leaders serve the organization like a fractal, setting the pattern through their values and behaviors, and through the extent to which they bring consistent alignment of the organizational vision with every aspect of the organization's work. As these patterns are set, and as people are allowed the freedom to repeat and build and expand on them, culture is born.

This same freedom keeps the steward leader from playing the owner. The freedom of the steward leader provides freedom for an organization to develop its culture. That is, although the fractal pattern is set, the way that pattern is expanded, duplicated, built on and arranged within the organization is the result of free people interacting in community. Wheatley writes, "Fractal order originates when a simple formula is fed back on itself in a complex network. And in true fractal fashion, these vital agreements do not restrict individuals from embodying them in diverse and unique ways."[14]

Steward leaders develop and nurture culture not by controlling information or manipulating perspective, but by modeling the heart of the steward leader and being free to allow it to be repeated throughout the organization.

> The potent force that shapes behavior in these organizations and in all natural systems is the combination of simply expressed expectations of purpose, intent and values, and *the freedom for responsible individuals to make sense of these in their own way.*[15]

Such an aim requires a leader to be free in her relationship to her job, her people and the vision of the organization, and to allow people to act freely as they develop culture.

If leaders serve like fractals to give shape and pattern to the culture of their organization, they must also understand that the culture transcends their leadership. We inherit culture wherever we go, and we leave it behind when we depart. If we are free in relationship to our organization and the culture we help shape, we must be able to walk away and allow the culture to change and reform under new leadership. Too many leaders cannot let go because, in part, they believe that the culture they have helped develop could not exist without them. This is nothing more than ownership and bondage dressed up in the guise of caring about the organization. While the leader may shape the culture, it is maintained, nurtured, developed, adjusted, amended and reformed by the community. In all of these ways culture transcends any one particular leader, and we need to be free from it in order to let that happen when it must. If we do not own the culture, we can allow it to be passed on to the next person God calls to lead. And when we look back and see that the culture we helped shape has changed under different leadership—under a new fractal pattern—we can rejoice in what God is doing.

Steward leaders who are truly free will neither underestimate the impact their behaviors and values have on shaping culture nor overestimate their own importance to its preservation and development after they leave. This is an important balance to maintain if we are to be stewards of our organizations at this first level.

Questions for Personal Reflection and Growth

1. Do you understand and appreciate the role you play in shaping and maintaining the culture of your organization?

2. What kind of fractal pattern are you modeling, and how is it being repeated throughout your community?

3. Is your community free to shape its culture according to the way God is leading it?

4. Where are you giving in to the temptation to play the owner-leader? Where do you need to ask for forgiveness from your people?

5. What is your next step as a steward leader in modeling the kind of freedom and joyful obedience on which your organization can develop a culture that glorifies God and builds the kingdom?

5

STEWARDS OF OUR
RELATIONSHIP WITH OURSELVES

LEVEL TWO TRANSFORMATION

The Steward Leader in the Mirror   Steward Leaders Develop Whole People   Steward Leaders Harness the Power of People

THE STEWARD LEADER IN THE MIRROR

While developing the concept of the steward leader, I have seen how often words need to take on new meaning. Never is that more the case than with our key word here: *confidence*. The word is immediately tied to its more common form, *self*-confidence—a term we must avoid as we discuss the steward leader at this second level. The problem with self-confidence is not that it focuses on us, but that it focuses *only* on us. Our confidence as a steward leader is built on a much broader and surer foundation than self alone.

To attain this confidence we need to start with two questions: What is the key motivator in your life as a leader? Are you free toward yourself? I will answer these questions as we look at the gift of confidence that is ours as the steward leader at this second level and at the temptation of self-confidence that will pull at us every day.

The Gift of Confidence

In chapter two I stated that because of God's self-revelation to us in

Jesus Christ, we have a real sense of certainty. This certainty is the basis for the gift of confidence, but it is not the same. Jesus Christ reveals to us the heart of God, the nature of our own identity and the purpose of our existence. This knowledge is not complete or perfect, but it is, as Karl Barth reminds us, "sufficient." It is all we need to know to live a productive, fulfilled and joyful life as God's people.

This certainty is the bedrock on which confidence is built in the steward leader. It must not be taken at face value but be truly internalized as a foundational statement of belief for every child of God. We *know with certainty* the heart of our God. We *know with certainty* our identity as a child of this God. And we *know with certainty* the purpose for our existence on this earth, at this point in history, in the place where we live. Our walk with Christ is an unfolding of deeper and deeper truth on all three of these levels, but what we learn will never contradict what we know today. It can only deepen, refine and expand this foundation.

That is the source of our confidence! We can stand in a volatile and shifting world and know in ourselves these three great, unshakable truths. The heart of God will never change: "Jesus Christ is the same yesterday and today and forever" (Hebrews 13:8); "I have loved you with an everlasting love" (Jeremiah 31:3). Our identity as image bearers of this God will never change. And our purpose in life—to love, serve and enjoy God forever—remains the same regardless of the variety of roles we play in life.

Our knowledge of this certainty, however, is not enough. For the development of confidence, the knowledge must be transferred into action. While I continue to affirm that being takes precedence over doing, it is in the doing that our being is developed even further. We can know in our heart that we have this certainty, but we are also called to step out in faith and live according to it. In living it out, our knowledge is deepened and our spirit is strengthened.

The gift of confidence is a gift enacted. It begins by making choices based solely on our supreme confidence in the heart of our Creator God. Steward leaders must do this personally before they can do it corporately. They approach life with a mindset that they are precious, loved, redeemed and blessed by the sovereign God of the universe. They will work each day, knowing that whatever momentary challenges may cross their desk, they are part of a grander story, the story of the working out of everything for their good (see Romans 8:28).

There is a threefold movement in this confidence: confidence in God's character, confidence in our role as his image bearers and confidence in our calling.

Confidence in God's character. While working recently on a novel,[1] from time to time I imagined what it would be like to talk to the main character as I developed his story. My keyboard took him to tough places, maneuvered him into frightening situations and brought him to the brink of absolute despair. Yet the whole time I knew the end of the story. I knew I could get him out of everything I had gotten him into, and I was always working things out around him for his well-being—most of which he wasn't aware was happening.

Had he cursed at me in times of despair, wondering why I had created him and why I wasn't taking better care of him (after all, I had the power to delete and rewrite), my response would have been, "Fear not, be still and know that I am the author. I created you, I love you, and your story is unfolding exactly like I intended. Just trust me and continue on, for I know how this ends, and you will definitely like it." This, I believe, would have instilled in my character a sense of confidence, assuming he believed me and trusted my heart.

Knowing the heart of our Creator God and believing in his daily work for our good in all circumstances is the steward leader's foundation of confidence. This leader will in turn lead others to rely on this same confidence.

On occasion I have watched in awe as a room once filled with tension, fear and despair was completely transformed as a result of one voice speaking a word of confidence. Steward leaders continually raise the eyes of their people to engage God's. They reconnect their people time and time again to their source of confidence. They do this naturally, because they personally reconnect themselves to that source, sometimes minute by minute.

Confidence as image bearers. There is a second aspect of this gift that is wholly dependent on the confidence we have in the heart of God. Godly stewards have been given the gift of certainty in their knowledge of their identity as the workmanship of this loving God, having been created in his image. This knowledge of their identity translates into the confidence that they were created to have a role in God's greater work. This is heady stuff! Our life is no accident.

Scripture sets up for us a tension in how we are to understand and steward this identity. I believe that understanding and maintaining this tension is the *single most challenging and important component* in the life of the steward leader.

On one hand, we are assured that we are a beloved child of God. We are "fearfully and wonderfully made" (Psalm 139:14). Our God has loved us with an everlasting love. We are truly "God's workmanship, created in Christ Jesus to do good works, which God prepared in advance for us to do" (Ephesians 2:10). Our lives have been bought with the blood of Christ so that we can be restored to intimacy and fellowship with the God who created us just to be with us. And we are *convinced* that "neither death nor life, neither angels nor demons, neither the present nor the future, nor any powers, neither height nor depth, nor anything else in all creation, will be able to separate us from the love of God that is in Christ Jesus" (Romans 8:38).

Steward leaders are certain that their Creator is a loving God, confident that they have been created as the special workmanship of this loving God and convinced that nothing will ever separate them from the love of their Creator God. That is the reality of the life of the steward leader on one side of this tension in how we are to understand and steward our identity.

The other side is just as real and certain. We are the redeemed yet still sinful children of God. For all the grace and love showered down on us, our hearts are still in need of the ongoing transformation of the Holy Spirit. We remain on the journey, and because we do, we still fall back into the old habits and sins of a life that is passing away yet still so very present. We are sinners in need of daily contrition, repentance and forgiveness. We fight against the flesh and a divided heart that wants so dearly to be obedient but listens so willingly to the siren's call to selfishness, greed and compromise.

We lament with Paul, "I do not understand what I do. For what I want to do I do not do, but what I hate, I do. . . . What a wretched man I am! Who will rescue me from this body of death?" (Romans 7:15, 24). Apart from Christ we can do nothing. We war against the flesh and fail often. We live in almost constant need of grace and forgiveness. Our sin separates us from intimacy with God, and once we are but momentarily separated from Christ (something we do, not him) we fall immediately into every sort of self-serving behavior. Such is the state of the child of God in this time between the resurrection and the second coming.

This, then, is the tension. Created by God for good works, and constantly doing the things we ought not to do. At once the new creation in Christ and a sinner in need of daily grace. Every day facing the need to die to sin and live for righteousness.

Our identity as godly stewards is found only in the very midst of this tension. As steward leaders we must carry this with us constantly, for when this tension is not maintained, we are pulled toward *self*-confidence on the one side or demoralization on the other.

Here it is enough to say that steward leaders lead from the center of this tension in their life and are thereby able to lead others to that same place. They can do this not only because they understand the tension and maintain the tension, but because it is in the right balance of this tension that they are free to lead. Freedom is not the result of the easing of this tension but just the opposite. We are free when we embrace both the wonder of our own creation and the depth of our sin. We are free when we know genuine humility in our need for daily repentance and grace, and genuine courage in our place in God's abundant grace and never-ending love. We are free to look our sin in the face and not let it overwhelm us. And we are free to let God work wondrous and miraculous things in us and through us without ever thinking that it is we alone who are wonderful and miraculous.

Steward leaders find this sweet spot, this place of maintained tension, and enjoy the freedom that God has for them there.

Confidence in our calling. Finally, steward leaders have confidence in their calling and their place in God's world. There is a general and a specific aspect to this confidence. The general part is the confidence that comes from the certainty that every minute of our life counts. There is no waste in God's kingdom. Our times of preparation, of reflection and of waiting are as dear to God and his purposes for us as our times of great accomplishment and productivity. God is the master author, and he is writing our story in all its dimensions. No author decides to fill lots of pages with a story line that is meaningless to the outcome (no good author, anyway). Every word, every event is part of the unfolding story. It all has meaning, and often the less dramatic moments carry the greatest weight. In our lives, God is at work in every moment. We are plugged into the greater plan, and our work is part of that plan. All our work has eternal value. Steward leaders carry that reality as they lead people experiencing the vagaries of life.

Yet we are also specifically summoned to exercise leadership in a specific place for a specific organization by serving a specific community of people. In this calling we can have the confidence that God is at work preparing us and the community for this purpose. God was at work in both spheres before we arrived and will continue his work long after we leave. For some duration we are stewards of this organization and this community.

When I was appointed to the presidency at Eastern Baptist Theological Seminary, they held an installation service and reception, inviting past presidents and other leaders to send letters of congratulations and advice. One former president shocked everyone by beginning his letter to me with the admonition "Don't plan to stay long." He went on to explain that good leaders get to work. They do not meander along relying on a long tenure. His advice was to be a faithful steward from day one, working not frantically but diligently and with purpose. He was right. Our specific calling to a role in God's kingdom comes with no guarantees of tenure. We must work with confidence that God will supply all our needs while we are there and then move us on when our work is complete (whether we see it or not).

The point here is that steward leaders are free in relationship to their specific calling. They can wear their mantle of leadership lightly. There may be no more dangerous person to an organization's health than the leader who *needs* the job. Steward leaders must be free to truly be stewards of the people they serve and the organizations they lead. They must reject every temptation to play the owner, and live and work daily in freedom with respect to their current position. This is not disengagement or aloofness, but real freedom. The alternative is seen in founders who destroy the ministries they built because they cannot see when it is their time to leave, or in leaders who have no identity beyond the job and so choose to stay well beyond their productive years.

Confidence in your specific calling means confidence in God's ability to move you to a new place of challenge and fulfillment in his good time. We need to be committed to serve our organizations with our whole heart *and* to be ready to leave it to our successors whenever God so leads, *both at the same time.* When we can accomplish both, we will know the freedom of the steward leader. Robinson writes,

> For me to navigate the waters of the humility paradox I have had to learn that confidence and humility are not inversely related; they are not opposite ends of a continuum. The theological basis for coupling humility and confidence is clear. In humility we acknowledge our gifts are from God. We have nothing to brag about. But our gifts are from *God.* What can give more confidence that that! In humility we acknowledge our utter sinfulness. But we have been redeemed by no less than the God of the universe. In humility we recognize that God's strength is made perfect in our weakness.[2]

The best tool leaders can have always at hand is a full-length mirror. Not for self-admiration but for self-examination. In it we look for signs of self confidence crowding out God-confidence. We look at our place within the tensions of our self-identity and examine ourselves for signs of having been pulled too far in one direction or the other. And we look for any erosion in our confidence in our general vocation in God's kingdom, or a slide into an ownership attitude in our leadership position.

This self-examination is the vital missing link in the sorry tales of so many fallen leaders. Author Michael Jinkins writes,

> Leadership finds our faults. The stresses of leadership probe us until our

weaknesses surface. Someone who has always deflected responsibility by putting the blame on others in times of stress will blame with a vengeance. Someone whose veracity is challenged will lie under duress. Graduate theological schools and ordaining bodies of churches must work together to help prospective pastors identify in themselves those areas of character that will undercut their ministries, especially in light of the fact that many of the character traits that are tolerated and sometimes rewarded in higher education are detrimental to congregational leadership. The most pernicious kind of naïveté is the naïveté about ourselves that keeps us from recognizing the seeds of our own destruction that lie in our hearts. The great leaders have recognized and wrestled with the fissures in their own souls. Poor leaders are always surprised by their weaknesses.[3]

The leaders who daily undertake such self-examination, who have "recognized and wrestled with the fissures in their own souls," aided by prayer and the accountability of faithful friends, have the greatest chance of serving the kingdom as true steward leaders.

The Temptation of Self-Confidence

If confidence is the gift and balance is the stewarding act, then *self-confidence* is the temptation. The enemy wants us to be anything but confident in the heart of our Creator God. He wants us to be anywhere but in balance in our self-understanding and perception. And he wants us to do anything but lead with freedom. His strategy is sleight of hand. He may not be able to keep us from being a child of God, but he will be happy to settle for making us ineffective in our work for God's kingdom. When we lose our confidence or place it in the wrong source, we become ineffective as godly stewards and as steward leaders.[4]

Let's look at two ways the temptation of self-confidence pulls at the heart of every leader: *discontentment and distraction.*

Discontentment. The gift of confidence in the nature and heart of God instills in us a sense of contentment. We are content to live our story because we trust its author. The sleight of hand that the enemy seeks to pull on us starts with a quiet questioning that eats away at this contentment. This started in the Garden. In the temptation of the first couple, we see how the enemy chose to use this shifting of focus to breed discontentment with the story line of their lives.

Satan did not call God a liar; he just eroded confidence in the first couple that the Creator had their best at heart. God had given them so much that was good, but perhaps he was keeping something from them. Satan did not say that God was not good; he just implied that he was not as good as he *could be*. As Adam and Eve listened, their confidence began to wane, and the possibility of a different and better story took hold in their hearts. Would a God who loved them want to keep from them this luscious fruit that would allow their eyes to be fully opened?

The enemy bred discontent in their hearts toward a lavishly gracious and loving God. The results were disastrous. For every believer, confidence in God's good intent for us and the contentment to live in the daily grace of God are the rock on which we stand. Because of what is at stake, the steward leader will be constantly tempted to question the stability and reliability of that rock. As those appointed to provide leadership to a community of imperfect people, steward leaders stand on that rock on behalf of, and sometimes in spite of, the people they lead. Often they stand alone. And sometimes they begin to question things that ought not be questioned. This is the seeping discontentment that the enemy seeks to work in us. The fruit of this discontentment is the temptation to step in and take care of things when God seems distant. We take control, make things happen, grab the wheel and steer. If God is not showing up like we want, it is up to us to take matters into our own hands. After all, isn't that just good leadership?

Resisting that temptation requires keeping a firm footing on that rock. When people are wringing their hands and raising questions about the presence of God and the direction of our leadership, we end up standing in a very lonely place. Perhaps that is why Paul talks of standing firm twice in his admonition to the Ephesians: "Put on the full armor of God, so that when the day of evil comes, you may be able to stand your ground, and after you have done everything, to stand" (Ephesians 6:13).

Watch for the seeds of discontentment sown in your life and the lives of your people. Steward leaders name the discontentment when they see it and constantly call their people back to the rock. As steward leaders called to trust and stand, may our song be the refrain from that great spiritual, "We will not be moved!"

Distraction. The second part of the temptation of self-confidence is distraction. I have portrayed the balanced life of the steward leader as a tension maintained between spiritual pride and self-abasement. I have said that at the heart of that tension lies the freedom of the godly steward to become the steward leader. Yet, as in any tension, there is a constant threat of moving too far to either side, throwing things out of balance and diminishing or destroying this freedom. This is the enemy's intent, and it doesn't matter on which side we err. The enemy is equally satisfied if we can be led to think more of ourselves or less of ourselves than we ought. Pride and self-doubt are equally destructive. When we are put off balance, we become ineffective and sometimes even counterproductive or destructive to the work of the kingdom.

The key to this balance, and the weapon against the enemy in this battle, lies in where we focus. Put another way, it lies in what we determine to be the ultimate source of our self-image, our identity. If Christ is our source, we see in him the reason for our confidence and the reminder of our dependence. As John Calvin counseled, we will look away from ourselves to Christ. The confidence can come to us only if Christ is indeed our sole source.

I mentioned earlier a bookmark that helped remind me of this vital truth. It read, "It doesn't matter if the world knows, or sees or understands, the only applause we are meant to seek is that of nail-scarred hands." That focus keeps a steward leader operating out of the freedom of a balanced self-awareness.

The temptation to distraction averts our eyes from Christ and has us look to any other source to secure our self-perception. Here again the tension of being and doing comes into play. As we focus on our doing, we tend to seek affirmation and find fulfillment from our work; as we do so, we shift out of balance. With our focus on Christ alone, our self-perception derives from the person we are in him, and we are freed from constant reliance on our success for our satisfaction. This is the fruit of the gift of confidence. The enemy is at constant war with us to keep us unbalanced, seeking affirmations and basing our confidence and our self-worth on anything and anyone but Christ alone.

Self-confidence and vision. I must say a final word about this temptation in light of a popular notion that leaders need to "own" the organization's vision. This idea stems from the belief that vision is embodied in the leader, and so there can be no room for compromise or doubt in the leader's heart regarding that vision. Only when the vision is owned, so the thinking goes, will the leader articulate it convincingly and work to carry it out effectively. The process does not stop there, but proceeds to infiltrate the entire community. We are told that we need everyone to own the vision, make it theirs and find their place in helping to achieve it. The thinking here is that when people own something, they value it and work to protect it and make it happen.

In my consulting career I have been guilty of climbing on this "own the vision" bandwagon. I never stopped to ask what it meant spiritually to achieve such ownership. When I finally did, I did not like what I found. I can point to several once-successful ministries brought to near extinction because their leaders owned the vision. And I can name leaders who are no longer employed at ministries they loved because they owned the vision.

Remember the ownership-stewardship tension. The steward leader is first a godly steward, and as such he or she has rejected all claims to ownership and has embraced a holistic understanding of the call to be a steward at all four relational levels. When the godly steward becomes a leader, this orientation to transformation carries over into the leadership role, and the steward leader emerges. How contradictory to have reached this point in the journey, only to be told, after all the work of rejecting ownership and embracing the mantle of obedient steward, that suddenly, when it comes to vision, he or she is to revert to the role of owner that had been so completely rejected.

When we own anything, we make it ours. By definition, things we own, we possess. You cannot own a vision for an organization and also be free in relationship to that specific vocational calling. You cannot make a vision your own and also wear the mantle of leadership lightly. Ownership is bondage, and owning a vision means being bound to it and the processes of achieving it. When we own a vision, it ceases to be God's and instead becomes *ours*. This is one small step away from developing self-confidence in our ability to achieve our own vision. And the temptation at this second level claims yet another victim.

When a community owns a vision, it just as disastrously becomes *theirs*. When leaders own visions, the achievement of vision becomes inseparable from the success of the leader. When communities own vision, the ability to listen to God's leading, to change, adjust and take a new direction, is diminished or even lost. This is *our vision* now, and we will put our heads down and work to get it done. I have seen organizations so fixated on an old vision that they believed was theirs, that they never looked up to consider a changing world or to listen afresh to God to test the vision, pray over it and amend it as necessary. They achieved their vision, but it was the wrong thing for their mission and its long-term health.

The point here is that steward leaders are stewards of the vision God places on the heart of the community. They must believe in it, be able to articulate it with conviction and work hard to achieve it, but they do this with the heart of a steward. Vision is entrusted to us as caretakers. As caretakers we need to keep in constant relationship with the true owner, willing and ready to shape and change the vision as directed by him.

The same is true for our community. A steward leader helps his people hear God's vision for them, articulates it in the community and plans to achieve it effectively. However, the steward leader also ensures that the ministry he or she serves is a listening community, always ready and open to hear a word of correction, adjustment and change. As such, the people, too, become stewards of the vision.

A Discipline: Daily Affirmation of Our Self-Image Within the Balance

Just as our first discipline requires daily prayer for a thirsting for intimacy with God, so our second discipline requires a daily self-examination to determine if we are living in balance and finding our confidence in Christ alone.

This is such a critical issue among leaders in the body of Christ that I want to share one more image with you. In John 5, Jesus comes across a man who had been crippled for thirty-eight years. The man is lying near the pool of Bethesda along with countless others. They all believed that an angel would come and occasionally stir the waters in the pool, and the first person who entered the pool after it was stirred would be healed. Jesus surveys the situation, comes to the man and asks him a remarkable question: "Do you want to be healed?" (John 5:6).

It would seem obvious to anyone that this man certainly wanted to be healed. He had been an invalid for thirty-eight years, and he now sat by a pool every day, trying to be the first one in whenever the waters were stirred. Wasn't it obvious that he wanted to be healed? Well, maybe not. Jesus was asking a heart question, not a health question. The crippled man avoided the direct question and instead shared his dilemma of being unable to win the sprint to the pool. He did not understand who Jesus was, and he therefore did not understand the real point of his question. Yet despite the man's answer, Jesus acted in compassion and healed him.

Self-confidence, which slowly shuts us off from God, is a sickness. It is actually a sickness unto death. It is an epidemic among leaders; we are too easily swayed into a mode of leadership that is self-serving, self-reliant and self-confident. True steward leaders are rare, and as soon as they believe they are that rare leader, they are already well down the path of self-centeredness.

Each one of us in any leadership capacity needs to be honest regarding this sickness. We need to name it for what it is and to practice the daily discipline of praying to be healed. We might, like the crippled man, choose instead to point to our situation as the reason we cannot be healed. "If only you knew my board." "If I just had someone who could raise money." "If the faculty would just support me." "If only I could hire the right people." And the list goes on. All the while Jesus stands by the side of the self-absorbed leader and asks, "But do you want to be healed?"

Do you? It is a necessary part of the ongoing transformation of the Holy Spirit as you are being shaped and formed into the person God created you to be—a godly steward who can also be a steward leader.

Daily discipline at this second level is a recognition of our need to be healed—healed of our self-confidence, our thirst for ownership, our excuses, our discontentment and our distraction. Pray for it every day, and watch God change your heart from self-confidence to God-confidence.

LEVEL TWO TRAJECTORIES

| The Steward Leader in the Mirror | Steward Leaders Develop Whole People | Steward Leaders Harness the Power of People |

STEWARD LEADERS DEVELOP WHOLE PEOPLE

I must resist the temptation to become formulaic or to fall back into offering methods and processes at this second level of trajectory. How you live out freedom and joyful obedience with your people is unique to you, your organization, your culture and the specific way in which the Holy Spirit will guide you into truth. I will be brief in these sections and only offer ideas of where this trajectory might lead you.

Steward leaders who are intentional about maintaining a godly balance in their life also intentionally desire for their people to develop and maintain a holistic, balanced life. Steward leaders can truly set their people free to see themselves as God sees them and love themselves as God loves them. What effect would it have on your culture, your morale and your organizational productivity if all members of your organization saw themselves in a balanced way, not thinking any better or worse of themselves than they ought? For most organizations I know, the impact would be transformational.

Steward leaders engender in people the gift of confidence and help them avoid or unburden themselves of the self-confidence that will eat away at their soul. This requires us to listen to and care about our people at a new level.

Consider the struggles you face in maintaining this delicate and crucial balance for yourself. What would it require for someone to help you? It would likely require a presence and intimacy difficult to develop in a work setting. Yet if we are watchful, prayerful and discerning, we will see clear signs when someone's self-awareness is out of balance. Steward leaders look for those signs and seek to cultivate relationships that allow for such deeper discussion. This may take place formally, as part of a performance review, or informally, depending on the level of trust and the openness of the other to let us pursue the issue.

Without doubt this can be risky and challenging, especially given our present-day fixation on privacy and the predominant postmodern misunderstanding of judgmentalism. As a steward leader, we are called first to model this balance and then to be discerning in helping our people pursue that same balance. Some may not want to be healed. Others may never let us in. However, we are responsible for our own faithful obedience to be godly stewards called to lead others to freedom. Although it may prove especially difficult at this level of relationship, we are called to it nonetheless. Let prayer and a winsome spirit lead us!

Here, as in the first set of trajectories, we cannot be different toward our people from how we are in ourselves. That inconsistency will show through eventually. This is why it is so critical to cultivate our own heart and undergo our own transformation as we seek to lead others. Max De Pree reminds us, "For many of us there exists an exasperating discontinuity between how we see ourselves as persons and how we see ourselves as workers. We need to eliminate that sense of discontinuity and to restore a sense of coherence in our lives."[5]

Molding versus unfolding. As we experience the transforming work of the Holy Spirit in us, we seek the same for our people. The process we enter into can be described as an *unfolding,* as opposed to a molding. That is, steward leaders seek to help people unfold the talents and character with which God has gifted them. Think of a flower in the spring. The more it is unfolded, the more beautiful it becomes. Every small movement unveils another hidden treasure. So it is with our people. As they are freed to see themselves as God sees them, and as they find that sweet spot of balance in their self-awareness, they begin to unfold before us. They become more useful to the Master, and they respond with joyful obedience.

This is in contrast to leaders who try to mold their people into shapes and sizes that best serve the organization in achieving its goals. Owner-leaders must maintain control over their people, and that includes the manipulation required to get them to do what the leader wants. The savviest owner-leaders play on the imbalance in people to their own ends. Developing people in this way means molding them into compliant followers who will do the boss's bidding without protest. Leaders who are not free will have no other option but to mold people into roles that will not threaten them. They will seek to bring down confident colleagues out of envy and fear, and they will keep those with low self-esteem exactly where they are. Owner-leaders are power brokers, and the less employees think of themselves, the more power is granted to the leader. This may seem extreme, but the temptation to take steps to rise above the people we lead is constant.

This is where our freedom is most critical to our calling. We must yearn for this freedom for those we lead. We must be so free in ourselves that we will lift up everyone who is around us.

> That's your obligation as a leader. When you're in the box, people follow you, if at all, only through force or threat of force. But that's not leadership, that's coercion. The leaders people choose to follow are the leaders who are out of the box. Just look back on your life and you'll see that's so. So your success as a leader depends on being free of self-betrayal. Only then do you invite others to be free of self-betrayal themselves. Only then are you creating leaders yourself; co-workers whom people will respond to, trust, and want to work with. You owe it to your people to be out of the box for them.[6]

We must be passionate about this balance for our people, so passionate that we take the risk of challenging the prideful in our ranks. They too are in bondage, and setting them free requires that we approach them with the heartfelt desire to see them unfold under the influence of the Spirit of God. We are willing to take the blows to see our people prosper, even if it means making hard decisions for them. Terminating someone's employment due to an unwillingness to address this imbalance may be the most ministering act we can perform if it leads him or her into a serious engagement with the root causes of the prideful behavior. Steward leaders must be able to put the well-being of their people first, even when their decisions seem to be doing the opposite.

A man I greatly admire told me the story of a moment that changed his view of leadership. He was struggling with the decision whether or not to fire a popular employee in his ministry. He had more than enough just cause, and deep inside he knew it was the right thing to do for her and for the ministry. Yet he could not bring himself to do it. Confiding his angst to a close friend and mentor he said, "I am so torn. I know I should let her go, but I just don't know what I should do."

"If you think you should let her go, why are you struggling so with the decision?" asked his mentor.

"Well, I am just thinking about what is best for my ministry."

What his mentor said next shocked him. "No you're not. I am sorry, my friend, but your indecision is not because you are concerned about your ministry. It is because you are concerned about *you*. This is a pride issue. What you are really struggling with is that some people will not like this decision, and as a result, they will not like you."

At that moment he realized that his pride *was* in the way. He considered what he would do if his reputation was not an issue, and the decision was clear. He needed to be transformed from being the owner of his reputation to being the steward of his people.

Herein lies a truth that provides more freedom than perhaps anything I have written on the steward leader. Steward leaders are not the caretakers of their reputation. In fact, they are called to be leaders of *no reputation*. Again, this does not mean bad reputation or questionable reputation, but simply *no* reputation.

One of the greatest bondages we can experience is the need to scurry around frantically and manage our reputation. If we hear a bad report about ourselves, we run and correct it. If we think someone has a negative impression of us, we are anxious until we can convince him otherwise. We worry about what people might think about us if we say we believe this or stand up for that. So we live in bondage to the fear that we will have our reputation tarnished by an inaccuracy or misperception. Owning that reputation and believing our self to be its caretaker is a devastating bondage. And the enemy will use it to manipulate us and scare us away from being effective for the kingdom of God.

We cannot set our people free if we are in this kind of bondage. Remember, our commitment as steward leaders is joyful obedience. We are called to obey God, whatever that means and wherever that takes us. All he seeks is a willing heart. If in our obedience some people think ill of us, so be it. If rumors are spread about us, we leave it to God to deal with it. If we are free in our relationship to ourselves, we are also free to let God be the caretaker of our reputation.

This desire for unfolding life in others influences our human resource policies, our hiring and management practices, our assessment and performance evaluations, our goals for our organization, and our measurements of its success—and ours.

Without balance modeled from the top, we cannot expect a transformational change in our people. That balance has implications for how we set and achieve goals, our desire for growth, our strategic planning and our evaluation and incentive systems. I know leaders who expect their people to work sixty-hour weeks, be available on weekends and make their work their highest priority. When employees take vacations or use sick time, these leaders carry silent resentment. They would affirm that God calls us to balance, but they do not practice it in their own lives, so they do not engender it in the people they lead.

We cannot say that we value balance and then set goals and expectations that require our people to live unbalanced lives to achieve those goals and meet those expectations. Helping our people develop and maintain the balance is a systemic challenge that needs consistent guidance from the heart of a steward leader.

| The Steward Leader in the Mirror | Steward Leaders Develop Whole People | Steward Leaders Harness the Power of People |

Steward Leaders Harness the Power of People

As the people we lead find greater balance in their self-understanding and unique calling, the organization as an organic system realizes an increase in organizational effectiveness, quality of work and employee satisfaction and retention. People are ready to perform at new levels of effectiveness when they have been set free to see themselves as God sees them. When prideful people find balance in godly humility and people with low self-esteem begin to understand who they really are as children of God, they are on a journey of transformation. The fruits of that journey are improved vocational performance, deeper levels of satisfaction and a desire for excellence.

Steward leaders help their people harness the energy that flows from this greater sense of balance and freedom. They not only help create the culture in which it can thrive but also provide the catalyst for its growth. When people are free, they want to work at a new level and achieve higher goals than before. Steward leaders lead the community to that higher place. Nothing can frustrate a person more than to have been set free to work as a godly steward, only to be forced to continue to work in an old system of bondage and ownership.

By harnessing the power of people, I mean creating systems that encourage and challenge people to perform at the highest level possible as an expression of their newfound freedom. Such systems involve *listening, agility and obedience.*

Listening. Steward leaders develop a culture that values the time, energy and discipline needed for listening carefully to those voices that can best guide and inform the organization toward achieving its goals. This starts with a passion for listening to God, which happens in a variety of ways across a broad range of institutional cultures. But it must happen diligently, frequently and overtly. Steward leaders develop systems that depend on the discipline of listening to the voice of God through Scripture, prayer, worship and community sharing, to name a few. It is done proactively and intentionally. It is not enough to ask everyone to "be in prayer" over certain issues. If we are to create a culture of listening, we must develop systems that bear witness to the value we place on listening. When people are freed from constantly listening to themselves, they are ready, as a community, to listen more carefully for the voice of God in their midst.

This listening broadens to include other voices that are critical for missional success, that is, listening to one another. We have more intelligence, creativity and insight right in our own people than we ever access. As people are set free in themselves, they are better prepared to be positive, creative and innovative voices in our community. Steward leaders encourage this, and the community serves as an incubator of ideas and innovation.

Listening may also include outside voices. Here is where the freedom of steward leaders is critical. They do not shy away from allowing outside voices of expertise and knowledge to be heard in the community. They are free to welcome the outside voices of consultants, colleagues from other organizations in your industry or conference speakers into your listening culture.

An actively listening community has the best chance of learning about best practices and evaluating its own work in light of them. It can see itself in a more realistic and honest way. It encourages creativity and rewards innovative thinking and personal expression. It is an extension of freedom, and it nurtures the journey of transformation that unites the steward leader with everyone he or she is privileged to serve.

Agility. Listening alone, however, is not enough. In fact, it can lead to frustration if people feel listened to but nothing happens as a result. For that reason, harnessing the power of people who have been set free must involve the creation of organizational *agility.* Again, this looks different for every organization. However, one common characteristic is the ability to adapt to new information in a time frame that allows the change to be effective. That is, change must be contextual. In this rapidly changing, interconnected world, agility may be the greatest attribute we can develop in our community. Again, it is a product of freedom. When we own a vision, we lose the ability to be agile. We cling to the vision and refuse to let go, even when all the signs around us tell us we should. When we are stewards of the vision, we understand that it may change and be reshaped according to critical information. Only an agile organization can make such a change and allow its vision to be recast as a result of a commitment to listening.

In my previous roles as president and consultant, I used to create five- to ten-year strategic plans. I abandoned that more than a decade ago. Now I create only three-year plans. That, too, may be on its way out. Imagine having created a comprehensive three- or five-year strategic plan in September 2008. Unless it was built on a highly agile platform, it would have been all but useless six months later, given the largely unforeseen national and global financial crisis. Instead, organizations are doing more scenario planning and creating more-flexible three-year plans that require ongoing listening and have built-in mechanisms for evaluation and adjustment. Such planning enables an organization to cast a vision for its future with confidence and to freely pursue adjustments along the way.

Owner-leaders like control and predictability. Change comes hard, and agility is not a valued characteristic in the owner-leader's organizational culture. They hang on to what is known and can be controlled, manipulated and confined. Lacking their own personal freedom, they cannot lead others in developing cultural agility.

When set free to live and work in a balanced self-understanding, people carry that personal freedom into a culture that can embrace a greater level of agility. And steward leaders harness that energy, empowering and encouraging their people to develop the kind of organizational agility that serves the kingdom of a God who invites us to follow him on a journey, not to exist at a destination.

Obedience. A final step is required in this process. An organization must not only listen and be agile enough to respond, but it must take also the final step and actually *obey* with its actions. I have seen healthy organizations listen carefully to the right voices, prepare their people for dynamic change and lead them to the edge of the new frontier, only to shrink back at the last moment and retreat to familiar territory. It takes great courage to lead an organization through a systemic change of any kind.

There are unseen risks and scores of interpersonal dynamics at work, constantly encouraging inertia. Even a free and empowered community faces obstacles when trying to be obedient to implement significant change.

A leader must be armed with confidence that the path the organization has chosen to travel is God's intention (listening); that it is has been well thought out and vetted with the best expertise available (listening); that the community has been prepared to make this journey (agility); that each person sees his place and role within that journey (agility); and that the motivation for the journey is absolute obedience. As they lead, they do not stop listening and responding. In fact, listening and responding with agility are signs of ongoing obedience. A cyclical, dynamic process reinforces the drive to obedience while it reshapes the form it will take.

Steward leaders harness the energy of a people set free through this dynamic process of listening, developing agility and responding obediently. There is no formula for how this looks in any given situation. It is a wholly Spirit-led process. These are just the contours of this trajectory of harnessing the power of your people. How it works in your organization under your leadership will be determined by your own process of listening, developing agility and responding obediently. Your job is not to know how everything will work itself out, but to lead your people in freedom that will result in joyful obedience.

Questions for Personal Reflection and Growth

1. Are you developing a listening culture in your organization? Are you open to listening to all voices speaking into your community?

2. Are you freely empowering your people to create organizational agility?

3. Are you obedient to God's calling to reshape and change your organization as he leads it on its journey?

4. How are you harnessing the energy and power of your people as they are being set free to serve?

6

STEWARDS OF OUR RELATIONSHIP WITH OUR NEIGHBOR

LEVEL THREE TRANSFORMATION

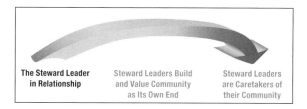

| The Steward Leader in Relationship | Steward Leaders Build and Value Community as Its Own End | Steward Leaders are Caretakers of their Community |

THE STEWARD LEADER IN RELATIONSHIP

Transformation at the first two levels dealt with the singular relationships of the steward leader to God and to him- or herself. At this third level—our relationship with our neighbor—we discover in an even more profound way the importance of understanding our created image as bearing the nature of our triune God.

Utilitarian relationships. We have affirmed God's triune nature as interdependent and mutually indwelling. That is, there is more, much more, to the triune relationship than the relationality we define in Western terms. Too often we see relationships as optional and highly utilitarian. We can choose to be in relationships or not, and when we do, we remain in control and use relationships to gain what we feel we need from them. This is not as heinous as it sounds. We freely enter into a friendship, and as long as we are both enjoying the relationship, it will likely continue. However, there is no requirement to stay in a relationship if one or both parties no longer believe it to be of value,

134 THE STEWARD LEADER

even the value of just enjoying one another's company. There is nothing malicious or necessarily self-centered about that idea. We simply choose not to spend our time in relationships that don't "work."

Unfortunately, this utilitarian view of relationships has spilled over into both the church and marriage. Here Scripture clearly tells us that the rules are different. In the covenant of marriage, we have the admonition that the "two become one flesh" (Matthew 19:5). This carries such a divine *imprimatur* that Jesus goes on to say that no one must undo what "God has joined together" (Matthew 19:6). Clearly there is a connectedness deeper than any other human relationship.

The same is true for the body of Christ. Jesus proclaimed us his body on earth. He prayed for our unity as that one body and told us our witness in the world would require that we work and live as one body. Paul continually unpacks the meaning of being one body with many parts. Here as well, the relationships within the body of Christ carry a far deeper meaning than the way we normally define *relationship.*

If we can affirm the uniqueness of both the marriage relationships and the interconnectedness expected as members of the body of Christ, what about our relationship to our neighbor? Does it, too, carry meaning beyond the casual and convenient? I believe that Scripture answers with an unequivocal yes.

Loving neighbors as ourselves. This third level of the transformation of the steward leader is based on the belief that the call to love our neighbor as ourselves is an admonition to see these relationships as being truly reflective of the image we bear of the triune God. It should be easy at this point in our study to follow the process already developed.

> Level one: We are in a unique relationship to God because we are his beloved creation, created in his image to have an intimate relationship with him as he transforms us into his likeness.

> Level two: We are in a unique relationship with ourselves because our identity is based solely on our understanding that we are God's workmanship, created to have balance and freedom as the Holy Spirit transforms us in our relationship with our self.

> Level three: We are in a unique relationship with our neighbor because

of our Lord's command to love our neighbor as we love ourselves, seeing in our neighbor the image of God and wanting to serve our neighbor in his or her ongoing journey of transformation.

If we are commanded to love our neighbor *as we love ourselves*, we must conclude that the relationship we have to our neighbor carries the same divine presence as the relationships at the first two levels. This means that the transforming work of the Holy Spirit continues in us that we might have the capacity and heart to love our neighbor.

The ethos of a community is fundamentally shaped by the depth to which its members are undergoing this transformation in love for their neighbor. Communities of casual, take-it-or-leave-it relationships will work always at the utilitarian edge. You know it as soon as you enter such an organization's workplace. You can feel it in the atmosphere. There is a distinct air of individualism, self-service and tolerance. Did I refer to tolerance in a negative way? Yes. Let me explain.

Scripture *never* tells us, commands us, calls us or even suggests to us that we tolerate anybody. In fact, the way we use tolerance in the West is an anathema to God and should never be the goal of any Christian. You see, I can tolerate your behavior, your beliefs, your race, your ethnicity, your sexual orientation and so on, and still hate *you* at the same time. Tolerance only asks that I keep my mouth shut, not act out against you and generally let you live the way you want. As long as I follow these rules, I will be viewed as a tolerant person. Yet in my heart I can still despise what you stand for, rejoice in your misfortune and never raise a finger to come to your aid.

So I can live as a tolerant person and please all of the rules of political correctness and have a heart filled with hatred toward my neighbor. And what is worse, I can and must (according to the rules of political correctness) let you proceed on happily in your sin without sharing with you the freedom God wants for all of us. For to share my journey and infer in some way that it is everyone's calling is to be absolutely intolerant. If ever there was a scheme hatched by a devious and hate-filled enemy, it is the worship of this sickly tolerance born of political correctness.

In the face of this charade Jesus gives us only one option toward our neighbors: to love them as we love ourselves. He rejects the easy option of outward grace and inward hate. There is no place for tolerance in the kingdom of God, only a true love for our neighbor that comes from the inward transformation of our heart. And we know that we cannot truly love our neighbor without that transformation.

The steward leader must be undergoing this transformation daily and, in turn, must lead his or her people on the same journey, person by person. The transformation starts with a definition of relationships, for when our understanding of relationships shifts from *means* to *ends,* nothing short of a transformation takes place.

The Gift of Presence

Our creation in the image of a triune God directs the form and function of our relationship with our neighbor. The form was established in the words of Christ, "Love your neighbor as yourself" (Mark 12:31). Given our transformation at level two, we can embrace the call to love our neighbor in the same freedom we have in loving ourselves. However, seeing our relationships with others as ends in themselves and not as means to some other purpose is a lot harder than it sounds.

Try to think of a relationship (not with a relative) in which you have invested a great deal of time, energy and emotion, and yet from which you have received almost nothing in return. Or worse, the return was negative. Yet because of the love you had for that person, you remained in the relationship and vowed to remain in it regardless of future behavior on his or her part. If you can think of one, I'll bet it is unique among your relationships.

This is a crude way of helping you get a feel for what it's like to care about another person without any requirements that the relationship ever bring you something in return. Taking a more realistic approach, think of your relationships that have waned or died out altogether. How many of them failed because the investment of time, energy and emotion brought little return? We may not want to admit it, but we tend to affix an expected ROI (return on investment) to each relationship we enter. If the return is not realized, we shift our investments to relationships with more potential.

The root of this problem is our bondage to self-interest. As long as we look to relationships to meet our needs or further our progress toward our objectives, they will always be measured by their utility. We will not make the shift from relationships as means to relationships as ends until we are personally set free. This takes us back to our progression: we are freed toward God that we might be free toward ourselves, and as we are free toward ourselves, we can love our neighbor as ourself, as ends and not means.

When we view relationships as ends and not means, we must use the gift of presence. We must be *with* people to be in relationship with them. This requires a prioritization of time, a commitment to involvement, and selflessness about our intentions and our desired outcomes.

Interdependence. This gift of presence beckons us into life as community. In community, we are not just individuals meeting together, but we are interdependent and mutually accountable and trusting. If we are the body of Christ, we are called to rely on one another, sacrifice for our neighbors' well-being and invest ourselves in community. We are called to reclaim the virtue and joy of sacrifice for one another and rediscover presence in a time-starved world. We do this understanding that our interdependence is a reflection of the image of our triune God. Yet we must also understand that, for some, this level of interdependence is a liability, not an asset.

Many years ago I was watching my eight-year-old son play basketball in a recreation league. I was sitting next to an overly zealous father whose identity seemed to hang on his son's every shot and dribble. At halftime we were talking about raising kids, and he commented that his goal was to raise his son to be completely independent. Without thinking, I blurted out, "That's interesting. I'm raising my son to be completely *de*-pendent." The man looked at me in horror and barely tolerated my meager explanation that we valued dependence on God greater than dependence on self. He never sat next to me again.

We will be called to lead many people for whom self-dependence and independence are valued and protected. They will not take quickly to a culture of interdependence, even if it proves good for business. So steward leaders not only need to help engender such a culture, but must also steward the limits of that culture and the expectation of those who populate it. The process of making it a reality in an organization (and even defining what that reality looks like) is the continued work of the steward leader.

According to Christ, our neighbors are gifts to us, and our relationship to them must be carefully stewarded. This stewarding is impossible without the Holy Spirit's ongoing work of transformation within us. We are being changed into the likeness of Christ, who calls us to a life of sacrificial service and unconditional love for our neighbor.

Steward leaders must make this shift first—and we may be the ones who struggle with it the most. After all, we hire people to get things accomplished. We train people for better performance. We reward people for achieving measurable goals, and we fire people for their inability to perform assigned tasks. We are in the business of getting things done through people, counting on the performance of others to help us meet organizational and personal goals. So how do we embrace such a radical transition in our view of our relationships?

It all goes back again to freedom and obedient response. Let me contrast the views of relationships in our organizations as seen through the eyes of the owner-leader (OL) and the steward leader (SL).

OL: I need to hire people who are top performers so we can make our goals, because my own performance will be measured by that standard.

SL: I want to hire people who will perform well because that will bring them satisfaction in their work, affirmation of their calling and success to the team.

OL: Judy is a rising star. I need to be sure she doesn't outshine me, or she might take my job someday.

SL: Judy is a rising star, and I will help her go as far as she can go, even if it means she takes my job someday. When God is ready to move me on, I will be ready to go.

OL: If Bill doesn't shape up, I'll fire him so he doesn't hurt the performance of everyone else and diminish my reputation as a tough leader.

SL: If Bill can't carry out his work effectively, I need to help him discern what God is saying and help him transition into a new job for his own satisfaction and for the sake of the team, which is counting on me to help all members find their areas of greatest giftedness and to support and serve them so that they can perform to the highest level of their abilities.

The shift happens in the heart of steward leaders who are free toward God, free toward their own self and therefore free toward the people they serve. This freedom requires the response of obedience. We are obedient by caring first for our people, trusting God to take care of us. This is not a call to a self-abusive, burnout style of leadership. We must love ourselves before we can love our neighbor. It is a call to the kind of selfless leadership that enables us to be stewards of our people and their skills, talents, aspirations and hopes.

High expectations. This shift has an impact on the level of accountability to which we will hold our people: it increases it! For God's people, who are called to do God's work, the stakes are high and the expectations are significant. Our work for our Creator God must be done at the highest level. He has created and equipped us for excellence, and we should expect nothing less of each other when we come together as a community to carry out God's mission. We will know real vocational fulfillment only when we are using our best skills in the best way to serve the kingdom of God. If we are doing anything less, someone who cares for us needs to tell us so.

Steward leaders must challenge underperforming employees at the personal level first. That is, they must help the employee understand how their current performance is not aligning with God's greater story for them. Or if it is, then a leader must find out what is happening in the employee's life to keep him from fulfilling his call and working to his potential. The impact on the organization is important, but secondary. If we believe that God is writing a greater story for every one of our people and that their work with us and for us is part of that story, performance issues need to be examined in that context. The shift from the owner-leader to the steward leader happens when we operate within that bigger picture and address issues in that context as a matter of course.

We will know in our hearts when we have made that shift, or when it is beginning to happen in us. Different thoughts go through our minds when we encounter our people in the hallway or at a meeting. We wonder what God is doing in their lives, where they are on their journey and what we can do to contribute to the work God is doing inside them. We pray differently. We ask that we might be a part of God's greater story for every one of the people we are privileged to serve. We pray for changed attitudes and for loving colleagues who will hold us accountable when we shift back into our owner-leader mindset. And we look at people differently. It is as if our eyesight has been altered. We are beginning to *see them as Christ sees them*. When and as that happens—as a process that is never completed—we can truly be their steward leader.

Leading in a secular environment. A word must be said to the steward leader who serves a secular organization or business. While the words used in discussions with employees must change, the attitude must be the same. If we are free toward our people, we still must ask the personal question first. Most everyone wants to be satisfied in their work, and a steward leader can help connect people to their area of greatest giftedness. Again the key here is the motivation. Everyone on this earth is on a journey with God in some way. And if we genuinely care about the journey our people are on, we will respond to them in that context. We will see them as Christ sees them and love them as we love ourselves. In a secular environment, while this may prove especially challenging day to day, it has incredible potential for the transformation of people. Even beyond this, it is your calling as a steward leader, regardless of the culture or spiritual context of the community in which you are called to serve.

Being present. The gift at this level is presence, and it is the fruit of this shift. When we have a proper attitude toward our people, when we embrace our call to be stewards of our relationships with them and begin to see them as God sees them, we want to and need to be present with them. There is no such thing as absentee steward leadership.

One regret I have from past leadership roles is the amount of time I spent in my office. I was not hiding, but I let administrative work take priority over relational work. I was less present with my people than I should have been. My reports were always on time, but many relationships around me were not developed in a way that conveyed my real love for those I served. If you love your people, you want to be with them. If you care about what God is doing in their lives and pray to be a contributor to their greater story, you must be with them.

Take the time to nurture the gift of presence. There is no substitute for it. In a time-starved world, presence always costs you something, and that is the point. You set priorities and sacrifice other things to be present with your people. They are gifts; steward them carefully.

The Temptation of Expediency

This temptation can be stated very succinctly: if it is our desire to use our relationships with others as a means to gain something we want or need, we will move from presence to expediency in our relationships. Remember earlier that I defined the enemy's attack on one-kingdom stewards as a temptation to build a second, earthly kingdom alongside our "spiritual" kingdom. The temptation plays on our desire to be owners, to have control and to chart our own course.

We respond by separating out a few things that were previously part of our submission to Christ, and we label these things "ours." They may be small things at first: our leisure time, our money, certain relationships and perhaps parts of our self-image. As we build this kingdom, we get reinforcements from the values of the world, which cheer us on and promise great rewards for those with larger kingdoms. So we quietly add items: our self-esteem, more of our time, our attitudes and most all of our relationships. The cycle continues until we are full-time owners and rulers of our own kingdom. When we bring our crowns to our place of employment, we immediately build our kingdoms with whatever materials we need and have available. For the most part, these materials are in the form of the people we lead.

Using others. Successful second-kingdom builders are experts at using people to get what they want. When you add the temptation to see the size of our kingdom as the source of our self-worth, you have the perfect storm. If we are in bondage to second-kingdom building, we place those under our authority in bondage to us. We need people to serve us if we are to achieve our goals. We measure their worth and the value of our relationship with them according to the level at which they serve us. Our attitude toward them is utilitarian, and our method is expediency. Get what you need, and move on.

This may seem like an exaggeration, but how many of us have worked for a superior we felt was concerned only about what we could *do*, not *who* we were? Even the best leaders in times of stress can revert back to utilitarian attitudes and owner-leader methods of operation. We must be careful to watch for those times when our view toward an employee has shifted and we revert to the expedient rather than the transformative. Sometimes we know it immediately; other times it comes on subtly.

Tragically, this temptation to use our relationships to get us what we want or need is too easily transferred from our vocational world to our private world. We can just as easily (and sometimes more easily) use our relationships with our friends, our children and our spouse as ways to get what we want and need in life, rather than ends in themselves that require our selfless presence. In fact, it is nearly impossible to so dissect our relational attitudes that we can be one person at work and another at home or church or among friends. If we are building a second kingdom at work, we are likely building it everywhere else as well.

Using God. The final distortion is when this use of others shifts to our relationship with God. How easy it is to take this final step and view God as a means to our own end. It affects our prayer life, our worship and our devotional life, and it erodes the foundation upon which everything else is built. Again, everything is predicated on our ability to be free toward God, freely knowing his love and freely accepting who we are as his image bearers. If we are back in bondage to the owner-leader mindset in our relationships with others, it will work its way back into our relationship with our self and finally into our relationship with God. We can actually attempt to use God to build a bigger kingdom for ourselves; such is the extent of the bondage that grasps at us.

As the image bearers of a God whose very nature is interdependent fellowship and community, we are in need of daily transformation to steward our relationships and to see them as ends and not self-serving means. We must pray for it daily and seek the Spirit's transformational work within us at this level as we seek to live out our calling to be stewards of these relationships.

A Discipline: Seeing Our Neighbors as God Sees Them

In truth we are all kingdom builders at some level. It is a temptation against which we must pray and work daily. We all use some relationships to get what we want. We all treat people we care about with expediency instead of presence. We all sense our freedom slipping away at times. These are signs of the need for the daily disciplines as steward leaders.

Change of vision. At this third level we must seek daily a change in our vision. We must pray that God will give us eyes to see and hearts to embrace the people in our world as God sees them and loves them. We must pray for a heart that seeks to contribute to the greater story that God is writing for each of them. As God answers that prayer, we will reject the temptation to expediency and more willingly make the sacrifice of time required of the gift of presence. We will see people as ends in themselves and call them to a level of accountability that reflects the very best of their God-given skills and giftedness. We will be free toward our neighbors, so that we might love them as we love ourselves.

Accountability. In addition to prayer, we need our own accountability. So the second part of this discipline is habitually inviting the trust and honesty of a group of people who love us and will covenant to walk with us on this journey. Steward leaders seek out and value accountability. They know themselves well enough to know that they need the love and honesty of friends and colleagues. When we are free toward God, free toward ourselves and free toward our neighbor, we are also freed to do the hard work of hearing the truth and continuing to submit ourselves to the transformational work of the Holy Spirit.

Pray for the mind of Christ and seek out accountability daily.

LEVEL THREE TRAJECTORIES

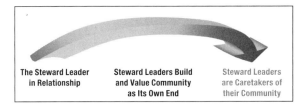

| The Steward Leader in Relationship | Steward Leaders Build and Value Community as Its Own End | Steward Leaders are Caretakers of their Community |

STEWARD LEADERS BUILD AND VALUE COMMUNITY AS ITS OWN END

This trajectory may present one of the greatest challenges for a steward leader. I have not written a great deal about the impact a steward leader may have on "organizational effectiveness," but here we must take on the challenge. Consider the following two scenarios:

Scenario 1: An executive director succeeds in creating in her organization a sense of true Christian community. People genuinely care about each other, and relationships are valued above everything else in the ministry. Time and resources are dedicated to maintaining and building this sense of community. As a result, employee morale, job satisfaction and retention are high, mutual respect and teamwork thrive, and a high level of trust and loyalty exists between employees and leaders. Yet overall the organization fails to meet its goals, suffers financially and is rated low on organizational effectiveness.

Scenario 2: A school superintendent has failed to create a sense of community in his school. People look out mostly for themselves, and everything is oriented around whether or not behavior and decisions will positively impact the school's bottom line. Employee morale is marginal and job retention is low. The employees know that their jobs are secure only as long as they produce and contribute to the school's financial health and further its mission. They are mostly concerned for their jobs and lack trust in leadership. Yet overall the school meets its goals, is financially stable and is rated high in organizational effectiveness.

How realistic are either of these scenarios? If we believe there is a significant causal link between community vitality and organizational effectiveness, neither scenario seems plausible. Of course, one major factor in deciding on this causal link is your definition of organizational effectiveness. And therein lies the challenge.

Defining success. Your ministry will be driven to a great extent by how you and your board, your staff and your clients define organizational effectiveness. However effectiveness is defined, everything will be modified to serve that definition. Whether achieving mission goals, gaining an increase in your number of graduates, seeing a decrease in the homeless population or any number of measurable outcomes, your definition of *success* is a critical determinant of your organizational life.

The question remains whether a leader will cultivate healthy communities as a *vital component* of organizational success, or only if it can be shown that it *leads to* organizational success. If scenario two is viewed as plausible, community will be regarded as subordinate to the outcomes. If the development of community is not essential to those outcomes, it will be regarded as expendable or at least as a low priority in the use of time and resources.

For the steward leader the question is *not* whether building and valuing community as its own end will *lead to* organizational effectiveness, but whether we are called to build and value community as its own end *regardless* of whether it leads to organizational effectiveness. We may even take the next step and say that if our definition of organizational effectiveness does not include such a community, perhaps it is our definition of effectiveness that needs to change, not the value we place on building such a community. We must ask ourselves what is normative in determining our definition of organizational success.

If we can agree that scenario two is an impossibility (especially in the long run) for a ministry whose greater purpose is to serve the kingdom of God, then what of scenario one? Is it possible to achieve this level of community health yet fail to succeed as an organization? Theoretically, we may say yes. However, in my twenty-seven years in not-for-profit life, I have never seen it. Perhaps the reason is that vibrant, trusting, healthy communities engender behavior consistent with almost every definition of organizational effectiveness. However, whether or not this is a provable position, we must force this discussion one step further.

Building community out of obedience. The reason steward leaders build and value community as its own end is not because they can prove a direct causal link with organizational effectiveness. It is not even because they have been able to include community as one value in their definition of organizational success. In the end, steward leaders build and value such communities because they are committed to joyful obedience to God's call to be godly stewards. They are not called to build such communities *so that* something may be achieved that looks like success. Steward leaders are obedient, period. That obedience compels them to love their people and to work in and through their people to develop communities that value relationships as ends. Success is measured in terms of obedience, not by a definition of organizational effectiveness or another standard of measurable effectiveness.

If this sounds detached from the reality of running a successful ministry, we must think again. Do we really believe that if we are obedient to God in building such a community, he will not bless it? He is the one who calls us as godly stewards to lead as steward leaders. He does not ask us to justify our obedience by human standards, but just to be obedient and to trust him for the increase.

But we must take this a step further. Do we believe that God created us to be at our very best when we are living in obedience to him? If so, shouldn't we expect that the most effective organization in kingdom terms will have this kind of community at its center? Why would God call us to build and value community as ends if he did not intend for such communities to be the very vehicles through which he would build his kingdom? If a kingdom definition of organizational effectiveness includes the development and maintenance of a healthy culture built on kingdom values, then we have proven scenario one to be an impossibility.

When we develop definitions for "success" and "organizational effectiveness," we must be very careful to ground them in thoroughly kingdom terms and according to kingdom values. Otherwise, if we borrow worldly standards, our misguided definitions of success might end up placing us in direct conflict with the very work we are called to do as steward leaders.

Building community in freedom and order. Building this kind of selfless, loving and serving community requires a steward leader and steward followers who are truly free. Only in freedom can a leader allow the room, the ambiguity and the trust necessary for such a culture to emerge. For the owner-leader freedom is a threat to control. Most all owner-leaders have a fear that, if people are given too much freedom, the result will be chaos. Owner-leaders believe people need order, control and boundaries; left to themselves, people will run amok. The steward leader will not deny that people need some sense of order and a set of basic ground rules within which to operate. However, freedom is a highly prized value, and steward leaders excel in granting it and protecting it. How else could one who has been set free lead others?

Freedom and order are the ingredients for the healthy communities we seek to build. Far from being mutually exclusive, these two characteristics are perfectly matched for the task of developing communities of trust, energy and mutual interdependence. Margaret Wheatley's work in studying self-organizing systems in quantum physics is helpful here.

> "The more freedom in self-organization, the more order." This is, for me, the most illuminating paradox of all. The two forces that we have placed in opposition to one another—freedom and order—turn out to be partners in generating healthy, well-ordered systems. Effective self-organization is supported by two critical elements: a clear sense of identity, and freedom. In organizations, if people are free to make their own decisions, guided by a clear organizational identity for them to reference, the whole system develops greater coherence and strength. The organization is less controlling, but more orderly.[1]

A steward leader can facilitate this because he or she is free to do so.

Here we see again the danger of owner-leaders who seek control as a means of establishing order. By trying to eliminate the risk of freedom and self-organization, they threaten the very life of the community they are called to steward. Life cannot be controlled. As much as we like to play the owner and exert heavy-handed guidance, we soon see clearly that we have far less control than we believe. As noted previously, Wheatley calls this living "off-balance."

All life lives off-balance in a world that is open to change. And all of life is self-organizing. We do not have to fear disequilibrium, nor do we have to approach change so fearfully. Instead we can realize that like all life we know how to grow and evolve in the midst of constant flux. . . . When leaders strive for equilibrium and stability by imposing control, constricting people's freedom and inhibiting local change, they only create the conditions that threaten the organization's survival.[2]

Although she does not come from a Christian worldview, Wheatley's work is interesting because she has discovered in quantum physics that relationships are the basic organizational systems by which all created matter exists.

She also provides a helpful comment on the importance of leaders— by any definition—standing in the midst of these relationships with people who allow us the extreme privilege of leading them.

Many writers have offered new images of effective leaders. Each of them is trying to create imagery for the new relationships that are required. . . . No one can hope to lead any organization by standing outside or ignoring the web of relationships through which all work is accomplished. Leaders are being called to step forward as helpmates, supported by our willingness to have them lead us.[3]

Wheatley's work has intriguing implications for the steward leader. By discovering relationality as the defining organizing system on which all created reality is based, she has reaffirmed the most central tenet of Christianity: that the Creator of the universe is a wholly interdependent, mutually indwelling triune God. A cosmos in which all matter is defined by its relational structure is exactly the kind of universe we would expect from a triune God who created all things *in his image*. And the four levels of relationship into which we were created are exactly what we would expect as the image bearers of this triune God.

Finally, the freedom Wheatley has discovered is the very foundation for how relational beings are to operate in a world created by a God whose greatest gift to us is the freedom to love him, love ourselves, love our neighbor and love the world he created for us. The tragedy is that for all of her groundbreaking work that fits so compellingly with a biblical and trinitarian understanding of our relational Creator, she has missed the most compelling and critical point by not seeing in this beautiful and complex creation the Creator himself. She marvels at the *handiwork* of the Creator but never marvels at *him*.

And so we must add to Wheatley's work here the all-important corrective that it is only through the transformation of the Holy Spirit and the redemption of all things in Jesus Christ that all other relationships in creation find their being, their meaning and their purpose. Without that basis we are thrown back on ourselves to discover that meaning without its defining reference point. And once again we find ourselves playing the owner and missing the opportunity for the joyful response of obedience and trust that is ours in Jesus Christ.

What this all means for steward leaders is that our work at building communities that value relationships as ends is an act of obedience that corresponds to both the triune nature of the Creator and the physics upon which his creation operates. While such communities may prove to be a critical component of organizational effectiveness and missional success, they are to be pursued and valued for much more than that. They serve as our greatest witness to the veracity of our faith and the extent of our obedience to the one of whom it is proclaimed,

> He is the image of the invisible God, the firstborn over all creation. For by him all things were created: things in heaven and on earth, visible and invisible, whether thrones or powers or rulers or authorities; all things were created by him and for him. He is before all things, and *in him all things hold together*. (Colossians 1:15-17, italics addded)

How will you, as a steward leader of your organization, build community that values relationships as an end? Will you hold such a process as your ministry's highest priority? Will you undertake this work through joyful obedience and trust God for the outcomes? That is your calling as a steward leader.

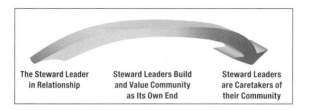

| The Steward Leader in Relationship | Steward Leaders Build and Value Community as Its Own End | Steward Leaders are Caretakers of their Community |

STEWARD LEADERS ARE CARETAKERS OF THEIR COMMUNITY

As organizational systems become more community-based, participants recognize the value of serving one another and valuing relationships as the basis of organizational health. Such organizations are more effective in meeting strategic goals and producing a stronger ROI (return on investment). Steward leaders understand their roles in nurturing this community in a variety of ways.

Michael Jinkins helps us understand a twofold responsibility, and tension, every leader faces. The tension is between the role of the leader as the representative of the organization's culture and the leader's role as the agent of change for that same culture. In Jinkin's terminology, the leader both *represents* the culture and *re-presents* it.

> This [tension] can place the leader in a moral dilemma. The leader—in order to accomplish this task of re-presentation—must almost inevitably second-guess the culture in question. This task requires a critical engagement of the leader with the organization and a distancing of the leader from the institution itself, as though the leader holds the organization at arm's length to bring it into better focus.[4]

Representing and re-presenting the culture. This description of the dual role of representing and re-presenting the culture is very helpful for the steward leader. Earlier I spoke about the nature of organizational culture to mirror or represent the values and behaviors of the leader. In the discussion of fractals we saw how the pattern that the leader embeds in an organization can influence the culture through the community's repetition of that pattern. Even when it is modified, adapted and changed (which every free organization should be allowed to do), it remains a reflection of the original pattern embedded by the leader. In this way, the leader represents the community and its culture.

Here we are considering how the steward leader is the caretaker of the community, which includes its culture. The above challenge reminds us that steward leaders need always to be able to find an objective stance with regard to their community in order to critique it. This distancing is possible only as a result of freedom. Owner-leaders are not *unable* to find such an objective viewpoint; they are *unwilling*. Owner-leaders want no part of critiquing the very thing they have dedicated their life to building. By identifying their own reputation and self-worth with the veracity and vitality of the community they lead, they eschew any attempt to call it into question.

I see this frequently in the process of strategic planning. When organizations, ministries, schools, churches and the like hire me to help them write strategic plans, one question that always arises is whether the CEO/pastor/executive director/superintendent should be part of the strategic planning process. My answer usually depends on the level of freedom that person has in relationship to the organization and its past, present and intended future.

I usually discover that level of freedom within moments of starting the strategic planning process. When an owner-leader is present, as soon as "weaknesses" are mentioned, a palpable unease fills the room. At this most critical moment, when the leader can play a vital role as caretaker of the community, he or she becomes the obstacle to that caretaking. The reason is ownership. Not only is the owner-leader in bondage to it, but so is everyone in the room, and probably everyone in the organization. The unwillingness and inability to take an objective, critical look at one's own organization is a clear indication that there has been a shift from steward to owner, and the response is bondage instead of freedom.

As caretaker of the community, steward leaders must be able to undertake this re-presentation frequently, systematically and comprehensively, and they do not do it alone. They need others to help check their perspective and expand their assessment. But they must lead this process freely and joyfully. They must repeat Kriegbaum's prayer, "This organization is not mine, it is yours."

Telling the truth. The next step in caretaking is the ability to tell the truth about what you see. It is not enough to take a critical look; you must see the truth and tell it. This is a harder responsibility than re-presenting. It is rife with temptations to see what you want to see and to shape reality according to your own preferences. Here again Jinkins is helpful:

> To lead effectually, the leader must be be-truthed. That is betrothed to reality. This commitment to grasp what is really the case requires other elements of virtue: courage, for instance, and flexibility. The leader of integrity is willing to face and to tell the truth even if the truth does not fit with personal preferences. . . . The leader who signals he does not have the integrity to face the truth will get the misinformation he deserves.[5]

Jinkins opens his book with one probing question: "What would it mean for leaders to concentrate on how things actually work in their organization rather than basing their decisions and strategies on how things ought to work?"[6] This, by the way, is the principle put forth by none other than Niccolo Machiavelli. Jinkins's book on character is a study of Machiavellian principles. Machiavelli's dogged adherence to seeing things as they really are and speaking truth about them is directed at us who are committed to be steward leaders.

There is an epidemic of non-truth telling when it comes to the state of our ministries and churches. Too often our trust in God's work gives way to sloppy accountability for our own work. We somehow believe that we are better off than we actually are because, believing that God is "on our side" regardless of how we operate. So we refuse to see the truth or speak the truth lest someone think us unspiritual. The result is a failure of leadership, organizational and community ineffectiveness, poor stewardship and lost ministry opportunities.

Steward leaders can be caretakers of their communities only if they are willing to take a careful, objective, critical look at their organizations, seek to understand the reality of their situation and speak the truth with integrity into the community to affect change. This entire process requires freedom at every point. If at any step the leader proves to be an owner, the process will either stop or be manipulated to meet the needs of the leader and not the community. Remember these words: "The leader of integrity is willing to face and to tell the truth even if the truth does not fit with personal preferences." That leader of integrity is the steward leader who has been freed to care for the community.

Questions for Personal Reflection and Growth

1. How do you faithfully represent your community?

2. How do you faithfully re-present your community?

3. From where do your obtain your objective viewpoint?

4. Are you free to see the reality of your community's strengths and weaknesses?

5. Can you speak truth into your organization freely without being influenced by your own sense of pride?

   Do you speak it?

7

STEWARDS OF OUR RELATIONSHIP WITH GOD'S CREATION

LEVEL FOUR TRANSFORMATION

| The Steward Leader in God's Creation | Steward Leaders Marshal Resources Effectively | Steward Leaders Create Organizational Consistency & Witness |

THE STEWARD LEADER IN GOD'S CREATION

We must consider God's creation in four aspects if we are to continue our commitment to transformation as godly stewards: our time, our skills, our resources and the created world in which we live.

"The LORD God took the man and put him in the Garden of Eden to work it and take care of it" (Genesis 2:15). Everything we possess in this world has come from the simple combination of the human being created in God's image and the Garden, which was created for the human, and the human for it. Those ingredients are the foundation for everything that exists in all of God's creation: a man, a woman and a garden. All of our advanced technology, our science, our music and literature, our civilization and global economy—everything grew out of the formula of man, woman and nature. Sometimes we make things too complicated. God says to Adam and Eve, "You love me and I love you. Cherish each other. Tend the garden."

Leading in freedom. It really is that simple for the steward leader.

God has not changed, nor have his simple commands. After the redemption of all things in Christ, God still says to us, "I love you and you love me. Love one another. Care for my creation." Is there anything in all the gospel that is not included in this simple statement? All four levels of relationship are here. Evangelism and world missions are here. Caring for the poor and working for justice are here. Creation care and stewardship of our money are here.

One of the great strengths of the steward leader is the ability to see complicated issues in clear and simple ways. Is there any issue today that could not be solved if we helped our people and our organizations love God more, love themselves more, love each other more and love God's creation more? Really, think about it. Is there?

On this fourth level we have an opportunity, like no other, to model for our people the freedom and absolute obedience of the steward leader. When you can truly be free from the lure of materialism and wealth, and the power and prestige they bring, you can lead others to freedom and joy. When you can stand in a peaceful relationship to time, neither serving it as a taskmaster nor wasting it as a sluggard, but enjoying it and investing yourself in it freely, you can free your people to accomplish incredible things for the kingdom. When you can stand in a free relationship to money as its steward, when God is the sole lord of your possessions and they hold no sway over you, you can set your people free!

Battling for creation. On this fourth level, like none of the others, steward leaders are in the battle of their lives. This is the enemy's territory. The Christian church has turned this arena over to him. With precious few exceptions, we have refused to deal squarely with the issues of money, possessions, time and environmental care. To our shame and detriment we have labeled these "things of this world" and have therefore shifted our attention to what we say are more "spiritual" issues. Of course, the enemy loves this. We have provided him perfect cover to ruin lives, distort truth, ravish God's beautiful creation and shackle God's people with back-breaking burdens all dressed up to look like material blessings.

The steward leader at this fourth level stands as a warrior in the battle for the heart and allegiance of God's people, starting with his own. Nowhere is the armor of God more vital than here. Nowhere will the steward leader experience the frontal attack of the enemy more than here. Plan for it, prepare for it and pray over it. We must be prepared for this battle personally, or we will never be able to lead our people to victory in their own battles.

Living as bearers of the image of God in the midst of God's good creation, we have a mandate to have dominion, rule over and subdue this creation according to God's vision for a redeemed world. For the steward leader, these words must be defined by the God who has created and redeemed this world and who calls us to be caretakers of it. We are called to love what God loves, and that includes his creation. This does not amount to a deification of creation. We are not required to embrace pantheism[1] or panentheism[2] in order to say that we love God's creation. There is no requirement to adopt Gaia worship, side with ideas of nature worship or animism, or be sympathetic to a latent Druidism to be an evangelical environmentalist.

These false expectations are cooked up by those who are afraid that if we love God's creation too much, we will divert our attention away from more "important" work like doing evangelism and supporting pro-life and pro-family issues. What they are missing is the interconnectedness (and how else would a triune God create us?) of these issues. What could be more pro-life than caring for the very creation that supports all life? What could be more pro-family than helping mothers and fathers be stewards of their time and financial resources, and passing those lessons and values on to their children? What could be more supportive of our evangelism throughout the world than to be able to connect the 78 percent of people who make their living from the earth to the God who created the earth through responsible creation care combined with the proclamation of the good news of Jesus Christ?

Steward leaders advancing on this fourth level will likely be shot at from both sides. We will battle with the enemy from without, trying to live free and uncontrolled in a world where money, possessions and power are all that matter. And we will battle an enemy from within, when those from our own ranks question our evangelical commitment because we have the audacity to love what God loves and to care for the creation, which was our original mandate, vocation, calling and joy. We will have to remind some of our colleagues that, according to Scripture, God's original intent was to hang out in a garden with a bunch of naked vegetarians.[3]

The steward leader will cultivate a heart that hears only the univocal call to one-kingdom living and will not be dissuaded by the cacophony of voices screaming to us the gospel of wealth, consumerism and consumption. Nor will the steward leader be persuaded by the authoritarian voices from our own ranks that can only see a world that is passing away instead of a creation that "itself will be liberated from its bondage to decay and brought into the glorious freedom of the children of God" (Romans 8:21).

To fight this good and worthy fight the steward leader is given the gift of nurture. The temptation is to forsake our role as nurturing stewards and to retake control.

The Gift of Nurture

Adam and Eve were charged to have dominion, rule over and subdue the earth *just as God* had dominion, ruled over and subdued them. The view from Genesis is that all creation was given to us as a gift to be nurtured. It is critical for us to delineate between God's definition of these words before the Fall and our post-fallen distortion where "dominion" becomes *domination*, "rule over" becomes *own and control* and "subdue" becomes *exploit*. A strictly post-Fall understanding of these words has yielded the grossly mistaken assumption that all the gifts of God are ours to use any way we want.

The gift of nurture is holistic, involving the entirety of God's good creation. This includes the stewarding of God's gift of time, God's investment in us of skills and talents that align with his calling, and God's provision for us through resources to meet our needs. This nurture requires that we are constantly being transformed as godly stewards, able to carry out the charge to have dominion, rule over and subdue as the very hands and feet of Christ.

To nurture means "to supply with nourishment, to further the development of."[4] If we apply this idea of nurture to the four areas of our study—time, talents, possessions and creation—we may be surprised by what we see.

Time. First, what does it mean to nurture time? Time was created when "there was evening, and there was morning—the first day" (Genesis 1:5). The rest of Genesis 1 and 2 tells of the creation of our world and the creation of humanity, placed in this world to tend it. The godly steward recognizes that our time is not our own. We have been given every second of life as a gift. It is not free, but neither is it burdensome. Time is a gift from God to be developed, nourished and cherished. What would it mean if we took seriously the value of every second of time? What if we did this, not with a franticness that measures value only in terms of doing, but in a more redeemed sense of desiring to invest every second in God-honoring ways? Can you nurture time spent in a grocery checkout line? Can you value time spent in a doctor's waiting room? Can you cherish time spent listening to your great aunt telling you the story you've heard a hundred times since you were a child?

The steward leader's relationship to time must follow the same two-fold vocational paradigm as we have followed at every other level: the steward leader is free in relationship to time and also responds to the use of time in joyful obedience. To be free in relationship to time requires a true steward's perspective. It means we lay aside the fear that comes from the sense that time is slipping away. It means we see the possibilities in the use of time as wonderful opportunities to be faithful stewards, to be creative and expressive and redemptive in our investment of this precious gift. To be free means that time does not control us. The clock is not our enemy, aging is not a plague, and deadlines do not rule our life. We are free to ask, "How would God have me spend this day, this hour, this lifetime?"

There was a certain lady who led a major foundation near Eastern Baptist Theological Seminary. I had spoken with her by phone on occasion, and finally I was granted a personal visit to talk about the seminary and our needs. I met with her in her office one sunny May afternoon, and we spent over two hours talking about the foundation and the seminary, but also about life and faith. It was a very enjoyable, if somewhat intense, experience. As we prepared to part, I asked if we could have a follow-up meeting. She agreed, and we conducted the usual business courting dance of comparing schedules until we struck upon a date and time that worked for both of us.

Satisfied that I had negotiated a suitable next step, I gathered my files in my briefcase and began to move toward the door. As she closed her calendar and placed it on her desk, she said to me in a most earnest tone, "Now, Scott, I need to tell you that even though we have a date and time on our calendars, I will wake up that day, present my schedule to God, and then ask God how *he* would have me spend my day. If he puts something else on my heart, I will have to call you and reschedule." I did the gracious thing and made some comment about how nice a process that was and how I would certainly understand if she needed to reschedule. I left her office, climbed on the elevator and, when the doors closed, I said out loud to no one but me, "Come on! Are you kidding? Who can live like that? How would you get anything done? This is absurd!" I left feeling justified in my incredulity over such a thing.

Since that day I have slowly come to realize that *she* was living in freedom to time and *I* was the one in bondage. She was free to use her time as she felt God was leading her, even if it meant inconvenience and frustration from people who lived as if their calendar was lord. But she was more than free, she was obedient. She didn't choose to write off appointments so she could use her time selfishly. She just wanted to know that every day of her life was spent as God would have her spend it.

---

*Are you free in your relationship to the
time God has given you?*

*Are you obedient to the way God would
have you invest that time?*

That is what it means to nurture the gift of time as a steward leader. As you do, you can lead your people in freedom in their own attitudes toward time.

Talents. When I think about freedom with regard to our skills and talents, I think about the balance I spoke of in our second level of transformation, the balance between spiritual pride and self-degradation. Balance here means that we rejoice in the skills God gave us and we have peace about the skills we lack. This does not keep us from honing our skills or developing new ones, but it does keep us from envy and jealousy regarding the skills of others. The enemy seeks to keep us in a state of discontentment regarding our skills in comparison to others'. He wants us to devalue our own skills and covet those we do not possess. Yet God has skilled us for the work he created us to do.

More than anything else in life, I love to preach. I am asked with some regularity to provide "pulpit supply" at our church, in some of the churches in our area and occasionally in other states. I see preaching the gospel as the highest privilege and consider it a great responsibility, and God has gifted me for this work.

On one particular Sunday I preached at our home church and relished the experience from start to finish. I left the church feeling fulfilled and humbled by the opportunity to share God's Word. That evening my wife and I had tickets to see a Broadway show that I had long wanted to see. Few people know that if I could come back in life as someone else (a wish borne of envy) it would be as a Broadway singer. I sang the lead in my high school musical and since that time I have secretly yearned to sing and act on Broadway. So as we watched the actors move the audience to tears with their incredible voices, singing powerful, memorable tunes, I felt in my spirit a growing discontent. By the time we arrived home, I was actually depressed, wishing that my skills had been different, my voice stronger and so on.

As I slumped into my chair, my wife noticed a voice message on our answering machine. It was my pastor. His message went something like this: "I just wanted you to know that there is a family in our congregation that has a foster son for whom they have been praying for years. Today, after they left church and got to their car, he said to them that something in your sermon had touched his heart, and he believed it was time to give his life to Jesus. They prayed for him right there and then called me with tears to tell me that this boy was now a child of

God. I just thought you might want to know."

I sat in my chair, stunned. All I could do was shake my head and say to myself, *You fool! How quickly you devalue the gifts God gave you to envy after others.* I learned that day the lesson of being a steward of my skills, thanking God for them, nurturing them and driving out any sense of envy or discontent.

Are you free in your relationship to the
skills God gave you, and to those he did not?

Are you obedient in using them in his service,
thanking him for them and rejoicing when you
see them used to carry out his work?

Possessions. The third area is our relationship to what we call our possessions. Even the term starts us in the wrong direction. To possess means to own, to exercise control over and to keep from the use and control of others. How do you "nurture" a possession? The answer is, you don't. You can't. What comes to mind is the loathsome figure of Gollum in Tolkien's *Lord of the Rings* trilogy. As he fondled the ring between his fingers, overwhelmed by the desire to possess it, he continually hissed, "My precious." In the end Gollum nurtured his possession to his own death. And, in a not too dissimilar way, so do we.

The godly steward's worldview transforms how the things of this world are understood and valued. Becoming steward leaders begins with being freed to be godly stewards, which means we were freed from the lure of ownership of things. We were called instead to nurture the physical stuff in our life in obedient response to its Maker. As steward leaders we must not fall back into old patterns of ownership and control. If money does not possess us, those who have it and can offer it to us will have no control over us. When we can nurture and develop the resources at our disposal while remaining free in relationship to them, we can lead others to freedom.

To nurture the things we possess is to always be reminded that we are temporary owners of them, never permanent or absolute owners.

They are forever at the disposal of their true owner, and so we can nurture them obediently and live lightly in relationship to them.

There are two biblical stories to be considered here. First, Jesus tells a parable about three servants who were given a sum of money by their employer prior to his leaving on a journey. When he returned, he asked about the disposition of his funds. Two of the employees had invested the money and made more, and to them he said, "Well done, good and faithful servant! You have been faithful with a few things; I will put you in charge of many things. Come and share your master's happiness!" (Matthew 25:23). The third employee had buried his funds in a hole, and when asked to give an account, he simply returned the original amount back to the master. The master was not pleased. He took the small sum and gave it to the employee who had the most, and threw the slothful servant out on his ear.

Interpretations of this parable vary, but for our study there are two very clear implications. First, we are stewards, not owners, of the material things we have and use. Our owner gives them to us and asks us to use them wisely while we have hem. When he returns, he will expect that we invested them well and can show a return. The account God will ask of us is one of obedience, not performance. That is, if the employees who invested the money had lost some of it, we can presume that the master would not have rebuked them, but appreciated the attempt to nurture the funds into something of greater value. The goal is not the amount of the return, but the obedient heart that is willing to make the investment. The unfaithful employee was not thrown out because he took the safe route, but because he chose a disobedient response to save his own skin.

Second, as steward leaders we are called to invest our possessions in the work of the kingdom. This brings up a difficult topic and, again, I may anger some colleagues by my comments here. It has to do with the building of endowments for our organizations. If we apply this idea of nurture and investment to the work of the kingdom, we are led to ask about the stewardship of tens of billions of dollars that sit in portfolios of major Christian universities and other organizations, earning 5 to 7 percent (and more recently, negative 7 percent), with small amounts taken each year for the ministry. When the Master returns, how will he respond? Will managers of these billions and the boards who hire them be praised for obedience in producing great results for the kingdom? Or will the Master look around at the thousands of faithful ministries that struggle desperately to fund their work while others sit on billions of dollars in safe bank accounts, and rebuke those who buried their talents in a hole while the needs of the kingdom went wanting? When Christ returns, do you want to be held accountable for an abundant ministry or an abundant endowment?

The second Bible story is a surprising lesson in the godly stewarding of our possessions.

> [Jesus] went on ahead, going up to Jerusalem. As he approached Bethphage and Bethany at the hill called the Mount of Olives, he sent two disciples, saying to them, "Go to the village ahead of you, and as you enter it, you will find a colt tied there, which no one has ever ridden. Untie it and bring it here. If anyone asks you, 'Why are you untying it?' tell him, 'The Lord needs it.'"
>
> Those who were sent ahead found it just as he had told them. As they were untying the colt, its owner asked them, "Why are you untying the colt?"
>
> They replied, "The Lord needs it." (Luke 19:28-34)

We know from the history of that time that a colt was a prized possession, one of the most valued possessions a household could own. It would one day serve as transportation, pull a plow, and carry items to market. In short, this young colt was going to play a major role in the health and prosperity of this family.

So these disciples come along and find the colt as Jesus had said and, as they were instructed, they start untying it and leading it away in broad daylight. The Scripture says that the owner sees all this happening and his response is a simple question, "Why are you untying that colt?" That may be what he said, but I think we might be missing *how* he said it. I think he likely picked up a stick and came running out at them, yelling in anger at the top of his lungs, *"Why are you untying that colt?!"*

All that the disciples say in response to the man's protest is what Jesus had instructed them to say: "The Lord needs it." The Lord needs it.

We assume that the owner of the colt knew who "the Lord" was and that the Lord was his Lord, too. And that is all that the owner needed to hear. What a response of faith!

The owner of that precious colt did not need a direct-mail fundraising letter. The disciples did not take out a brochure and say, "Well, this colt is part of the Triumphal Entry Campaign. As you'll see here, according to our Table of Gifts we need five contributions at the 'colt level,' and we are hoping you would consider giving one of those today." They offered no plaque on the walls of Jerusalem, no seat next to Jesus at the major donor banquet. "The Lord needs it." That is all the disciples said to this angry man brandishing a stick. And upon hearing those words, the man just let it go. What a marvelous picture of a heart tuned to God! Imagine what it must have been like for that man in a few short hours to see the King of kings and the Lord of lords riding triumphantly into Jerusalem *on his own colt.* [5]

I love this simple example of a person giving sacrificially for the right reason and then seeing the amazing things God does with that gift. That is what it means to nurture the things of this world and hold on lightly to our possessions. That includes our organizations and all of their trappings, including endowments, facilities and reputations. It includes buildings and budgets, offices and ornaments, perks and privileges and power. We are stewards of it all and owners of none of it. We are free to nurture it and obedient in response to how we invest it. And we lead others in that same freedom and obedience.

---

*How are you investing your possessions
in the work of God's kingdom?*

How free are you in relationship to your possessions?

*Where do you hear the voice of the Spirit saying to you,
"The Lord has need of it"?*

Creation. Finally, we come to the nurture of God's creation as a steward leader. Here I will be brief, not because there is little to say but because there is so much to say. This is a larger subject than I can manage in the scope of this book. (For more reading on this topic, see appendix two). At the intersection of the call to freedom and obedience as a steward leader and the global environmental crisis, we face an enormous, overwhelming challenge. To nurture creation at this point in human history is simply not enough. We are in an all-out battle to save it. Our opportunity for nurture is gone. If we do not act boldly, we will destroy this world—and ourselves with it.

This has profound implications for the steward leader. It will affect everything, from how we build new buildings to how we choose our food providers, from what we will do with acres of lawn around our buildings to how much travel we will choose to do to conduct business. If we are first stewards of God's earth, then as steward leaders we will find countless ways to lead our organizations in the care of that earth. We must do this as ones who stand free from an animist sense of some ontological unity with creation and also as ones who are absolutely obedient to the God who created us and who calls us to nurture and care for this earth. This is not an option for a steward leader. It is mandatory! Care for creation is not one choice on the smorgasbord of Christian living. It is basic to our very being as the children of God.

To nurture God's creation in this day and age requires us to be outspoken and proactive in transforming our organizations to conform to the very best in sound environmental practices. It starts with our own attitudes and habits and then permeates our organizations.

How are you personally involved
in nurturing God's creation?

In what ways does your organization
bear witness to our call to be caretakers of the earth?

Does your organizational commitment carry over to your
budget, your policies and your procedures?

Do you have a personal and a corporate
theology of creation care?

Steward leaders nurture creation itself, their time, their skills and their possessions, and they lead their people and their organizations in the same freedom toward the same obedience.

The Temptation of Control

More than at any other level, this fourth one is where our kingdom-building tendencies tempt us the most. The root of this temptation is our desire for control. Simply put, nurture is other-centered while control is wholly self-serving. This is a struggle for lordship! We want control because we can use it to serve ourselves. We grow up believing that there is nothing scarier than being "out of control." As we grow wiser, we learn that there may be nothing more terrifying than the consuming desire to be in control of everything.

In twenty-seven years of working in ministry, I haven't encountered any force more damnable than the desire to gain control of every sphere of life. We believe that with control comes security, power and peace. We seek security in our ability to use control to shape and manipulate things so they turn out our way. We believe that with enough power we can force solutions and mandate outcomes to our own liking. And we can then find peace in our ability to know what is good for us and create a world that produces that good.

Of course, this is all a clever and heinous deception. When we actually have even a small portion of that power, we totally mess things up. We find out that our solutions are not always healthy or empowering, our manipulation produces results that we did not expect or want, and the peace we craved ends up even further from us as a result of our lunging for it through our wielding of power. The call to nurture involves time, talents and possessions, and so we will face the craving to control in each area.

Trying to control time. When we seek to control time, we are proved a fool. Time is a cruel taskmaster, and the more we seek to control it, the more it laughs in our face. Try to slow things down, control how fast time passes or make it yield to your own goals and timelines. Impossible! Yet the enemy keeps whispering in our ear that we need to control time or it will run away with us. And so we end up in bondage to the time we seek to control.

Both our freedom in respect to time and our bondage to it seem to show up most readily in our planning processes. I have led strategic planning for dozens of ministries over the past decade. The tension that always emerges can be defined as hearing God's voice and discerning God's vision on one hand, and just listening to ourselves talk on the other. The one reliable indicator that has helped me guide my clients in deciphering these conflicting voices is this idea of freedom with respect to time.

Here is how it works. When plans are made as a result of listening to our own voices, they are accompanied by a certain anxiety about time. That is, the time lines that are created generate anxiousness and concern. There is an ominous tone to the consequences of missing milestones or failing to keep on schedule. Simply put, there is little freedom with respect to the measurable deadlines that are contained in plans that we generate by listening to our own voices.

A group gains a different sense after having created a plan that is a faithful response to hearing God's voice. That plan has just as many deadlines and measurable goals, but there is a palpable peace that permeates the process. It is based on the conviction that if this is truly God's vision for us, we begin a journey with him in accomplishing it. That journey may take us in a lot of directions that we cannot see today, *and that's okay.* This is God's plan, his timeline, and he will lead us through it in his time and in his way. Far from engendering a lackadaisical response, it calls us to the highest levels of commitment and requires of us our very best work in pursuit of the vision. There is an absence of anxiety over the timing of the work when people are both freed and called to passionate, obedient response.

The enemy will seek to enslave us to time in the mistaken belief that somehow we can control it for our own use. As steward leaders, we must resist this temptation for ourselves first, then for our people and our organization.

Trying to control talents. The same bondage awaits those who seek to control God's gift of skills and of possessions. When we try to control our skills and abilities, we become pretenders. We pretend we are skilled for certain things when we know we are not. Yet envy and jealousy will push us to depend on our weaknesses and to rely on our deficiencies. What an incredible gift it is to be free in the way you view other people's skills in relationship to your own. Yet it does not come cheaply. It is a constant battle against our desires for control.

Leaders who have not won this battle will destroy the people with whom they work. I wrote earlier that the most terrifying boss you can have is someone who really *needs* the job. A close second is the boss who cannot allow anyone else to excel in areas in which the boss is weak. Everyone can spot a pretender. We cannot lead effectively if we are constantly trying to prop up our image and work in areas of our weaknesses. It may be easy for us as leaders to write this off as not our problem. But be careful; this is a deceptive temptation. Envy toward the skills of coworkers and jealousy toward their accomplishments is subtle and insidious. It bubbles up from a desire to control.

Steward leaders have the ability to celebrate the victories of others without envy. They reject the temptation to manipulate their work to steal credit from others who are more skilled for the task. They rest secure in how God has gifted them and rejoice when they see how others excel in areas where they are less skilled. This is real freedom.

Trying to control possessions. Finally, control of our possessions may bring the greatest heartache. So much is expected of stuff that returns so little. When we shift from steward to owner, we vest in inanimate objects a sense of power that will ultimately control us. How ironic that our desire to control stuff results in our bondage to that same stuff. At this point the submission of the godly steward becomes the freedom of the steward leader. We must understand the reciprocal relationship of submission and control, and of freedom and bondage. This relationship applies to all four levels, but it is experienced here more than anywhere.

Simply put, when we submit something to God, we are immediately freed from it. When we wrest control of anything for ourselves, it immediately enslaves us. Think about it.

Are you free in relationship to your finances?

How about to the budget for your business or ministry?

*Do you carry the burden for your fundraising success,
or have you submitted it to God, and been set free?*

Carrying burdens. We carry burdens only for those things we control. And we control those things that we seek to have as part of our own kingdom, where we are lord. Lordship and ownership, control and burden—they are a package deal. In some forms, they look very spiritual. We can carry the burden for our organization, believing that somehow, if we suffer when things go badly, we are bearing the burden for others. Yet this is a gross misunderstanding of what it means to carry the burden for someone else.

Paul speaks of carrying the burdens of others when he writes, "Carry each other's burdens, and in this way you will fulfill the law of Christ" (Galatians 6:2). The point of this verse is *to fulfill the law of Christ.* What is the law of Christ? It is freedom! "For the law of the Spirit of life set [you] free from the law of sin and of death" (Romans 8:2). "But the man who looks intently into the perfect law that gives freedom, and continues to do this, not forgetting what he has heard, but doing it—he will be blessed in what he does" (James 1:25).

We carry one another's burdens as a sign of our freedom, not our bondage. In doing so, we fulfill the law of Christ, which is the *law of liberty.* When Christ calls us to this beautiful, sacrificial act of carrying the burdens of others, the enemy slides in alongside us to convince us that they are really *our* burden. When we listen and make it our own burden, we foster both spiritual pride and real bondage.

Are you are a champion "burden-bearer," feeling often that you are the only one carrying this whole load for your organization? Have you felt that small sense of spiritual pride that accompanies such a magnanimous act? Do you also live with the effects—spiritual, physical, emotional, relational—of the daily strain of toting around the load? Then listen to the words of Jesus, who bore all of our load for us: "Take my yoke upon you and learn from me, for I am gentle and humble in heart, and you will find rest for your souls. For my yoke is easy and my burden is light" (Matthew 11:29-30).

The only burden we are asked to bear is the one we bear in freedom in his name and for his glory. Every other act of burden bearing is a counterfeit. Are you free with regard to your possessions, including your finances and those of your organization? You must continually submit to God whatever would seek to burden you down. As you do, you are continually set free.

A Discipline: Daily Submitting to the Lordship of Christ

Richard Kriegbaum writes the following in his leadership prayer concerning ownership:

> This is my one incessant prayer to you, hour by hour, day upon day: It's yours. I am not fighting this battle for you, God. It's your battle, and you are fighting it for me. It is all yours, and I want whatever you have for me in this situation. It is not my organization, it is yours. So I depend on your Spirit to show me what to do. These are not my people. I chose them and organized their efforts, but they do not belong to me. . . . So this day is yours; I am yours; these people are yours; the resources are yours. The challenges we face are yours, as is anything we hope to accomplish. It's yours, God. It is not mine.[6]

I encourage every leader to pray this prayer every morning. It is a prayer of freedom. It is the level of complete submission that we must all yearn for if we are to be steward leaders for our people and our organizations at this fourth level.

Watch for the signs of your attitudes slipping into an ownership/ control mindset. You will know it by its companions: fear, anxiety, compulsion, envy, mistrust, selfishness and impatience. These are signs that you have stopped submitting and started grasping, controlling and seeking to play the owner. They are bondage.

The daily discipline must begin before we leave our bed. It is the awakening prayer that follows our praise to God, our thanks for the day and our placing of loved ones into the care of our loving God. The next prayer we must pray is this one: "It is not mine, it is yours."

Don't leave your bed without it! Once we start the routines of our day, our ownership and control tendencies come rushing in. We need to enter each day in freedom, prepared to live in joyful obedience. This is especially true at this fourth level, because the tendencies to revert are so natural in our psyche, our attitudes and our habits. To break the cycle of ownership and control, we must not leave our beds until our hearts are free. It is easier to reject a temptation in our freedom than to unburden ourselves of it when it has already climbed aboard.

Set your alarm ten minutes earlier. Leave your Blackberry off and your laptop shut. Guard your mind from intruders. "Take captive every thought to make it obedient to Christ" (2 Corinthians 10:5). "Prepare your minds for action" (1 Peter 1:13). "Put on the full armor of God"(Ephesians 6:11). And pray this prayer of submission to God. Do not leave your bed until you are overwhelmed with the love of Christ and sense the freedom he wants for you.

You may need to keep this prayer close at hand and pray it often throughout your day. Memorize it, along with the Scripture verses above. Discipline yourself to recognize bondage attitudes and attack them at the onset with the freedom of absolute submission. Claim the promise "It is for freedom that Christ has set us free" (Galatians 5:1).

LEVEL FOUR TRAJECTORIES

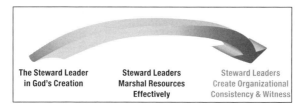

The Steward Leader in God's Creation — Steward Leaders Marshal Resources Effectively — Steward Leaders Create Organizational Consistency & Witness

STEWARD LEADERS MARSHAL RESOURCES EFFECTIVELY

For all my work at refraining from offering formulas and methodologies in these trajectories, I must not fail in this final section. It is so tempting here to talk about processes for helping your organization be greener or ways to improve the use of your land, buildings and endowment. When we start talking about *stuff*, it is easy to get specific and tactical. However, even here—and I could say *especially* here—we need to continue to rely on the discerning work of the Holy Spirit to guide us into processes and policies unique to our community and its mission.

What I can say is that if the Holy Spirit is leading the process, it will be holistic and transformative. That means it will include the stewarding of your organization's time, talents and resources. It will not be selective or politically correct. It will likely impact every person in your organization, and it will require you to think in new ways, ask different questions and consider alternatives that may never have been on your radar screen.

When steward leaders look across their organizations, study their budgets, review their policy manuals, walk their properties and check their garbage, they are led through this process of thinking differently.

Stewarding time. It should start with a new assessment of your organization's stewarding of time. Ask yourself how well you lead your ministry regarding time. Does your community convey a sense of being both free in respect to time and joyfully obedient in its use of time for the work of the kingdom? Do your human-resource policies reflect this balance in how employee time is managed, rewarded and valued? Where is time wasted, and where does the community demonstrate an unhealthy bondage to time?

Some leaders may undertake a "time audit" of their organizations to help answer these questions. For communities in bondage to time, this can be a threatening process. However, until people are set free, institutions and their systems remain in bondage. And if only individuals are set free, they will never be able to operate at their true potential if the systems that govern them continually throw old shackles back on them. Both individuals and institutional systems must be freed if an organization is to use its time effectively for the work of the kingdom.

Steward leaders take seriously their responsibility to be stewards of the way their organization uses time and the way time is understood and valued. And they use strategic planning as a tool of their stewardship.

Few leaders would say that they have ample time for their people to achieve the goals they have set for themselves or time to accomplish the mission of the organization. Few if any employees would say they have plenty of time to do everything required of them. We all take pride in our overwhelming busyness. Yet it is a false and deceiving pride.

The tyranny of time drives many good pastors from the ministry and many good leaders from the head office. We set unrealistic goals within too short a time frame and rely on too few resources to accomplish too large a task. We do this believing that somehow this makes us look like we have great faith compared to those with more modest objectives. When we fail or burn ourselves out in the process of "succeeding," we look back and wonder where we went wrong. Some blame God for not showing up. Others blame themselves for underperforming or over-promising. In the end, it is often just a matter of poor stewarding of the institution's time, which can be traced to poor planning.

Effective strategic planning starts with a realistic assessment of the balanced and God-pleasing employment of the time we have been given for our task. Frantic and anxious activity belies poor planning. Yet many hold up such behavior as a badge of honor. I know leaders who expect their top people to work at a pace that can result only in an imbalance in their life at every level. These hard-driving leaders somehow believe that God will honor and bless a schedule that leaves precious little time for family, spiritual growth, physical care and rest. They work their people as if time was their enemy, and it inevitably becomes so.

Leaders who are not free with respect to time, who carry a sense of ownership of their organization and who tie ministry success to their reputations will invariably lack balance in their life, treat time like a great thief and drive their people to do the same. They may be able to point to a list of accomplishments, but the cost to their people is enormous.

Steward leaders develop strategic plans in a context of what is achievable given a God-pleasing use of time. They pray hard to keep any vestige of pride and ambition from the planning process. If there was ever a time for a leader to say the prayer, "It's not mine; it's yours," it is during the strategic planning process. Often, effective leaders push their organizations to dream bigger, set their sights higher and dare to risk and step out in faith when they plan for the future. This is fine and appropriate as long as the leader is truly a *steward* leader who is free in his or her relationship to the organization and its future, and who challenges his or her people as an act of pure obedience. Such a leader will always seek to set goals and take risks within a commitment to a God-pleasing use of time. However, if the heart of the steward leader shifts to owner-leader, the strategic planning process can be used to raise the reputation of the leader, who has tied self-image to the outward success of the ministry.

How do you steward the time of your organization, and does your planning bear witness to a God-pleasing view of time?

Stewarding talents. Steward leaders will employ that same freedom in their use of the skills and talents of their people. I mentioned the notion of enabling an *unfolding* of your people as whole persons. Here this idea develops in how the steward leader plans to use the best skills of every person in his employ.

The steward leader also helps people excel in ways that transcend their own beliefs about their capabilities. If you have ever experienced significant growth as a result of great leadership, you know that steward leaders stretch us, challenge us and make us better at what we do. They help us discover new talents and develop our abilities to the highest level possible. They put us in situations where we can rely most often on our most reliable and effective abilities, and in doing so we find not only success but also satisfaction. All this is a stewarding of our people's talents. It is a process of continually encouraging their unfolding.

Here again the steward leader can use effective strategic planning as a tool in the efficient employment of people's best skills, matched to their best application. By its very nature, strategic planning seeks to match the best resources of an organization to the most important issues that will determine its long-term vitality and growth. In writing plans we ascertain the strengths and weaknesses of ministries to develop goals that build on the former and overcome the latter. When we write objectives to address our goals, we assign them to the people uniquely skilled to achieve them, and we provide the resources for those people to be successful.

Marshaling the right people to do the right jobs with the right resources to achieve the right goals at the right time is one of the highest callings of the steward leader. And for that reason, effective strategic planning is one of the highest forms of organizational stewardship.

Stewarding resources. Finally, steward leaders marshal physical resources effectively. This is where the commitment to be a godly steward comes with a radically new set of lenses when the steward is called to lead. Nothing looks quite the same, and that includes the physical resources at our disposal. Buildings, endowments, land and other such resources require our best work as stewards. This can result in some pretty unusual actions. Colleges plow up lawns to plant community gardens. Churches turn Sunday school rooms into everything from job training centers to addiction recovery facilities. Seminaries build facilities that serve as both student residences and low-income housing for their neighborhood. Ministries tithe from their endowment. And the list goes on and on. Again, two tools that can be helpful are a resource audit and a well-designed strategic plan.

The process, however, starts in the heart of a steward leader. It was just such leadership that helped bring about the recent American College and University Presidents Climate Commitment, which united dozens of Christian colleges and universities in a commitment to climate neutrality. Similarly, the Evangelical Pastors Creation Care Covenant is setting similar goals. These are signs of steward leaders taking seriously the call to joyful obedience in marshalling their resources effectively for the kingdom.

As a leader, how well do you marshal the resources at your disposal?

What criteria do you use, and how do you measure the outcomes of your decisions?

God gives us freedom in relationship to these resources that we mighty employ them effectively through a process of joyful obedience to his calling. We are called to be faithful and to trust him for effectiveness, blessings and return.

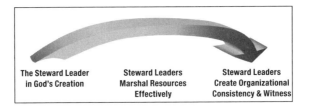

| The Steward Leader in God's Creation | Steward Leaders Marshal Resources Effectively | Steward Leaders Create Organizational Consistency & Witness |

STEWARD LEADERS CREATE ORGANIZATIONAL CONSISTENCY AND WITNESS

This final trajectory provides an opportunity to summarize what has come before. I will close this study by lifting up two final aspects of the work of the steward leader: consistency and witness.

The thought of implementing these trajectories across all four levels may seem overwhelming. Each has layers of complexity that need to be interpreted prayerfully and applied caringly within your organization in the specific ways that the Spirit leads. This a huge task for anyone. Yet we must remember that all God asks of us is our obedient response, and I add here that such a response will be consistent.

If we are being transformed into godly stewards at all four levels, we should expect to lead with consistency as we seek to be faithful to our calling as steward leaders on all four levels. This is not pick-and-choose, smorgasbord leadership. That is why I have rejected a trait-based approach or a ten-step process for good leadership. Such models and processes are seldom holistic, and they can lead to inconsistent application.

This entire study has emphasized the holistic nature of the steward leader. Therefore, we should expect that the work of the steward leader will have an internal consistency. The power of this consistency cannot be overstated. The potential for compromise is ever-present when an organization seeks to be a consistent steward according to God's plan. The temptations to ownership and control call to us every day, and when we succumb, we look like hypocrites. This is why consistency and witness are so closely linked.

Our job as steward leaders is to strive for consistency in our organization, and it begins with us. This takes us back to the very beginning of this study. Our internal transformation is a lifelong journey. It will have its victories and its backsliding. However, the further we journey, the greater the victories and the more infrequent our missteps. We grow and mature as godly stewards, and we bring that to our work as steward leaders. As we live more consistently as one-kingdom stewards, we lead the people we serve and the organizations we lead in the same consistency.

This consistency means we work at transformation at all four levels. There is no hierarchy or priority. Some will be easier for us than others, but all four are indispensible if we are to reflect the image of God in which we were created. Where do you struggle the most in living out consistently your call to be a godly steward? It is likely that at this same place you will struggle to lead your organization consistently as a steward leader.

Remember the concept of fractals from quantum physics. Our organizations repeat the patterns and values we instill. From that repetition come our culture and the values of our community. If we set up flawed patterns, or patterns that are deficient in one area, the community will reflect this through its inconsistency. Fortunately, we have godly colleagues, accountability and the ongoing working of the Holy Spirit to provide correctives. It is not all up to us. However, we must take seriously this role of the steward leader and understand how significantly our own lack of consistency as a godly steward will impact our organization and our witness.

Steward leaders must be brutally honest with themselves in knowing their own weaknesses and addressing them. For some, this requires accountability. For others, it means the practice of disciplines that include self-assessment and honesty. For all of us, it requires a daily "dying and rising": dying to the sin of control and ownership that leads to bondage, and rising in freedom to the life of the godly steward. As we do this daily, we isolate those areas where we are most vulnerable to our kingdom-building tendencies. Then we can name them and, through prayer, call all the resources of heaven to combat them.

Your people cannot expect you to be perfect as a person, but they must be able to trust you to be consistent as a leader. And they need you to help them to be consistent as a community. This is where the community can serve as a partner with the steward leader. Steward leaders empower their people to look for inconsistencies and work for solutions. The relationship between the steward leader and the people he or she serves is based on unfolding, empowering, lifting up, challenging and rejoicing.

I have said consistently that steward leaders are united with their people on this journey of faith. As such, they develop their people as holistic stewards, see them as ends and not means, and employ their skills in ways that bring them fulfillment and joy. This egalitarian understanding of the role of the steward leader serves that leader well when it comes to the challenge of organizational consistency. Involve your people, seek accountability and develop the value of consistency as central to your mission. As your people journey further in their transformation as godly stewards, they will become ever more vital partners in cultivating and maintaining organizational consistency in living out the call to be holistic stewards as a community.

CONCLUSION

Beyond the successful achievement of our mission and our strategic goals, God calls us as individuals and as faith communities to be witnesses in this world. We must never forget this overarching responsibility. We do not serve the kingdom of God if we meet our strategic goals but do so in a way that bears witness to worldly values and secular measurements.

If we build our success on poor stewarding of our people's time and talents, we have failed in our call. If we claim victory in a capital campaign when the world sees manipulation and coercion as our tools, we have built in vain. We can become the false spiritual facades of which Jesus said, "You are like whitewashed tombs, which look beautiful on the outside but on the inside are full of dead men's bones and everything unclean" (Matthew 23:27).

How many fallen leaders fit this description? When they failed to allow the Holy Spirit to do the internal work of transforming them into a godly steward, they became owner-leaders. When they failed, their organizations paid a heavy price, but the greatest damage done was to the reputation of the kingdom of God. All the frontal attacks by atheists and Christ-haters in the media and literature combined have done less damage to the witness of the body of Christ than Christian leaders who have failed to live consistent lives as godly stewards.

In October 2008, we experienced the beginning of a major economic collapse, due in large part to the greed of financial leaders in our banks, investment firms and regulatory agencies. One of my colleagues knew

I was writing this book and had read a summary version of its main points. He called me and said, "Scott, write fast. We desperately need steward leaders!" And so we do. What is at stake in our Christian ministries and churches is not just missional effectiveness but transformational witness.

What does the world see when it looks at your ministry—not its brochures, videos and annual reports, although those are important, but when they talk to your employees, walk your grounds, attend your events, listen to your board members and view your work in your community with other leaders and organizations? What do they say about you when they see you at your daughter's soccer game, encounter you in a slow checkout line at the grocery store or drive behind you on the freeway? Consistency and witness are integrally tied. If the enemy cannot make us unfaithful, he will try to make us ineffective. And we lose our effectiveness as steward leaders when we model inconsistent behavior and allow our organizations to do the same. What we lose is our witness, which means we bring shame on the name of Jesus Christ.

This final admonition points once again to the damage that can be done by the owner-leader. If you are attempting to lead while in bondage to the need to control, you *will* fail. Your organization will falter, and you will do damage to the witness of Jesus Christ in this world. Those are very high stakes! This is why throughout Scripture God consistently called men and women who loved him to leadership. They were anointed before they were appointed. They sought his face before all else. And they succeeded not because of their abilities, but because they were God's man, God's woman. Yahweh is looking for those whose eyes are looking back toward heaven, those with whom the Spirit can make eye contact. For this reason, the first level of our created relationship is intimacy with God. And we are back to the start.

This daily intimacy arises as the very core from which the steward leader leads. It is the beginning point on the journey of transformation. It is God's deepest desire for us. The great church father Irenaeus proclaimed, "The glory of God is man fully alive."

And so I return to the questions I posed at the outset of this journey:

- Are you prepared to go deeper in your faith than you have ever gone before?

- Are you ready to be used by God in more powerful ways than you ever thought possible?

- Do you desire to bless the people you serve and the organizations you are called to lead?

- Are you ready for the journey?

That is your calling, your hope and your promise. God can make you fully alive as a godly steward who responds with joyful obedience in every area of life. I would add to Irenaeus's quote, "The glory of the kingdom of God is the leader who is completely free." Through such a leader, God can do great things for the kingdom. And chief among them is the consistent work of a community of godly stewards who bear witness to the world of the transformational work of the Holy Spirit in their lives. The result is a community fully alive. To God be the glory!

A SUMMARY OF THE FOUR DISCIPLINES OF THE STEWARD LEADER

Level One Discipline

Praying for a Restoration of a Thirst for Intimacy
Every day of the life of a steward leader must begin with a thirst for intimacy with God. Pray for it, cultivate it, repent of the obstacles you have placed in front of it, expect it as a gift from God, and celebrate it when it is found. This thirst is a gift, but it must be sought and received.

Level Two Discipline

Daily Affirmation of Our Self-Image Within This Balance
The daily discipline at this second level is the recognition of our need to be healed—healed of our self-confidence, our thirst for ownership, our excuses, our discontentment and our distraction. Pray for it every day, and watch God change your heart from self-confidence to God-confidence, the heart of the steward leader.

Level Three Discipline

Seeing Our Neighbors as God Sees Them

At this third level, we must seek daily a change in our vision. We must pray that God will give us eyes to see and hearts to embrace the people in our world as God sees them and loves them. We must pray for a heart that seeks to contribute to the greater story that God is writing for each of them. In addition to prayer, we also need accountability. So the second part of this discipline is the trust and honesty of a group of people who love us enough to walk with us on this journey. Pray for the mind of Christ and seek out accountability daily.

Level Four Discipline

Daily Submitting Every Aspect of Our Lives to the Lordship of Christ

This is my one incessant prayer to God, hour by hour, day upon day:

> It's yours. I am not fighting this battle for you, God. It's your battle, and you are fighting it for me. It is all yours, and I want whatever you have for me in this situation. It is not my organization, it is yours. So I depend on your Spirit to show me what to do. These are not my people. I chose them and organized their efforts, but they do not belong to me. So this day is yours; I am yours; these people are yours; the resources are yours. The challenges we face are yours, as is anything we hope to accomplish. It's yours, God. It is not mine.[1]

I encourage every leader to pray this prayer every morning. It is a prayer of freedom. Our daily discipline must begin before we leave our beds. It begins with this simple prayer: "It is not mine; it is yours." Don't leave your bed without it! Discipline yourself to recognize bondage attitudes, and attack them at the outset with the freedom of absolute submission to the triune God of abundant grace.

---

[1]Richard Kriegbaum, *Leadership Prayers* (Wheaton, Ill.: Tyndale House, 1998), pp. 6-7.

APPENDIX 1

FAITH-BASED LEADERSHIP STUDIES
BY FOUR POPULAR WRITERS

Bennis, Warren. *Managing People Is Like Herding Cats.* Provo, Utah: Executive Excellence, 1997.

———. *Managing the Dream: Reflections on Leadership and Change.* Cambridge, Mass.: Perseus, 2000.

———. *Reinventing Leadership: Strategies to Empower the Organization.* New York: Collins Business Essentials, 2005.

———. *Beyond Leadership: Balancing Economics, Ethics and Ecology.* Cambridge, Mass.: Blackwell Business, 1994.

———. *The Unconscious Conspiracy: Why Leaders Can't Lead.* New York: AMACOM, 1976.

———. *Why Leaders Can't Lead: The Unconscious Conspiracy Continues.* San Francisco: Jossey-Bass, 1989.

———. *An Invented Life: Reflections on Leadership and Change.* Reading, Mass.: Addison-Wesley, 1993.

———. *Leaders: The Strategies for Taking Charge.* New York: Harper & Row, 1985.

———. *On Becoming a Leader.* Reading, Mass.: Addison-Wesley, 1989.

———. *Learning to Lead: A Workbook on Becoming a Leader.* Reading, Mass.: Addison-Wesley, 1994.

———. *Transparency: How Leaders Create a Culture of Candor.* San Francisco: Jossey-Bass, 2008.

———. *Geeks & Geezers: How Era, Values, and Defining Moments Shape Lead-*

ers. Boston: Harvard Business School Press, 2002.

De Pree, Max. *Leadership Is an Art*. New York: Broadway Business, 2004.

———. *Leading Without Power: Finding Hope in Serving Community*. San Francisco: Jossey-Bass, 2003.

———. *Leadership Jazz*. New York: Dell, 1993.

Drucker, Peter. *The Effective Executive*. Ann Arbor: University of Michigan Press, 1967.

———. *Peter Drucker on the Profession of Management*. Boston: Harvard Business School Press, 1998.

———. *Managing in the Next Society*. New York: Butterworth-Heinemann, 2007.

———. *Management Challenges for the 21st Century*. New York: HarperCollins, 2001.

———. *Managing the Non-Profit Organization*. New York: Butterworth-Heinemann, 2004.

———, et al. *Leading in a Time of Change*. San Francisco: Jossey-Bass, 2001.

Engstrom, Theodore Wilhelm. *The Essential Engstrom: Proven Principles of Leadership*. Colorado Springs: Authentic, 2007.

———. *Compassionate Leadership*. Ventura, Calif.: Regal, 2006.

———. *The Making of a Mentor: 9 Essential Characteristics of Influential Christian Leaders*. Waynesboro, Ga.: Authentic, 2005.

———. *The Fine Art of Mentoring: Passing On to Others What God Has Given You*. Brentwood, Tenn.: Wolgemuth & Hyatt, 1989.

———. *The Christian Leader's 60-Second Management Guide*. Waco, Tex.: Word, 1984.

———. *Seizing the Torch: Leadership for a New Generation*. Ventura, Calif.: Regal, 1988.

———. *Your Gift of Administration: How to Discover and Use It*. Nashville: Thomas Nelson, 1983.

———. *The Making of a Christian Leader*. Grand Rapids: Zondervan, 1976.

———. *The Art of Management for Christian Leaders*. Waco, Tex.: Word, 1976.

———. *The Christian Executive: A Practical Reference for Christians in Management Positions, Leaders of Christian Organizations, Christian Educators, Pastors and Other Christian Workers*. Waco, Tex.: Word, 1979.

APPENDIX 2

A SELECTION OF WORKS ON NURTURING GOD'S CREATION

Basney, Lionel. *An Earth-Friendly Way of Life.* Downers Grove, Ill.: InterVarsity Press, 1994.

Brown, Ed. *Our Father's World.* Downers Grove, Ill.: InterVarsity Press, 2008.

DeWitt, Cal. *Earth-Wise: A Biblical Response to Environmental Issues.* Boca Raton: CRC Publications, 1994.

———. "Three Biblical Principles for Environmental Stewardship." Au Sable Institiute Online Resources <http://ausable.org/or.resources.online.7.cfm>.

Kirk, Janice and Donald. *Cherish the Earth.* Waterloo, Ont.: Herald Press, 1993.

LeQuire, Stan. *The Best Preaching on Earth.* Valley Forge, Penn.: Judson Press, 1996.

Robinson, Tri. *Saving God's Green Earth.* Boise: Ampelon, 2006.

———. *Small Footprint, Big Handprint.* Boise: Ampelon, 2008.

Van Dyke, Fred, et al. *Redeeming Creation.* Downers Grove, Ill.: InterVarsity Press, 1996.

Check out <www.creationcare.com>, <www.coolingcreation.com> and organizations like Restoring Eden, ARocha, the Au Sable Institute and Floresta.

Also see declarations on Christian environmental stewardship and a call to action at <http://www.baptistcreationcare.org/node/1> and <http://www.creationcare.org/resources/declaration.php>.

NOTES

Part 1: Becoming a Steward Leader of No Reputation

[1]This chapter is adapted from an article by the same name that was first published in *The Journal of Leadership Studies*, Vol. I, by R. Scott Rodin (2002).

[2]Henri Nouwen, *In the Name of Jesus* (New York: Crossroads, 1996), p. 17.

[3]David McCullough, *John Adams* (New York: Simon and Schuster, 2001), p. 19.

[4]Nouwen, *Name of Jesus*, pp. 62-63.

[5]Robert K. Greenleaf, *The Servant as Leader* (Westfield, Ind.: Greenleaf Center, 1970), p. 7.

[6]Stephen R. Covey, *Principle-Centered Leadership* (New York: Fireside, 1990), p. 61.

[7]Max De Pree, quoted in James O'Toole, *Leading Change* (New York: Ballantine, 1995), p. 44.

[8]Among the many authors who are championing the cause of careful self-awareness are James O'Toole, Stephen Covey, Noel Tichy, John Kotter, Peter Block, Warren Bennis, Max De Pree and Peter Drucker.

[9]Greenleaf, *Servant as Leader*, p. 34.

[10]Nouwen, *Name of Jesus*, pp. 29-30.

[11]Richard Kriegbaum, *Leadership Prayers* (Wheaton, Ill.: Tyndale House, 1998), p. 22 (italics added).

[12]Nouwen, *Name of Jesus*, p. 60.

Chapter 1: Leading in the Image of the Triune God

[1]I am indebted to theologian Karl Barth for the understanding of the sufficiency of our knowledge of God for faith and life.

[2]Augustine *Confessions* bk. 1, p. 1.

[3]See, for instance, Ephesians 1:3-10; Hebrews 4:1-3; 1 Peter 1:17-20. These and other verses, combined with the overarching theme of the election of all humanity in the eternal Son, support the theological position that God's intended purpose to save humanity in Jesus Christ was in place before creation, and so his covenant with us and his sacrificial love for us predates our very creation.

[4]Karl Barth, *Church Dogmatics,* trans. G. W. Bromiley and T. F. Torrance (Edinburgh: T &T Clark, 1956), 4.1, p. 436.

[5]This concept of our being "life-givers" in our creation in the image of God was developed in February 1998 by John Kinney, the 1998 Mitchell Lecturer at Eastern Baptist Theological Seminary.

Chapter 2: The Freedom of the Steward Leader
[1]Dietrich Bonhoeffer, *The Cost of Discipleship* (New York: Macmillan, 1948), p. 73.
[2]Hannah Whitehall Smith, *The Christian's Secret of a Happy Life* (Grand Rapids: Baker, 1952), p. 163.
[3]William Robinson, *Leading People from the Middle* (Provo, Utah: Executive Excellence, 2002), p. 220.
[4]Tri Robinson, *Small Footprint, Big Handprint* (Boise: Ampelon, 2008), pp. 90-91.
[5]Arbinger Institute, *Leadership and Self-Deception* (San Francisco: Berrett-Koehler, 2002), p. 106. This is a very helpful book, written as fiction. If its approach could be translated into Spirit-led transformational language, it would be a great asset for the kingdom.
[6]Ibid., p. 123.

Chapter 3: The Distinctiveness of the Steward Leader
[1]I am indebted to Mark Vincent and his comparative work on leadership theories for this section.
[2]James MacGregor Burns, *Transforming Leadership* (New York: Grove Press, 2003), p. 11.
[3]Ibid., p. 24.
[4]Ibid., p. 26.
[5]Ibid., p. 29.
[6]Bernard Bass provided his own description of transformational leadership, taking a different stand from Burns, primarily on the motivation of the leader. Bernard M. Bass, *Bass and Stogdill's Handbook of Leadership* (New York: Free Press, 1991).
[7]Margaret Wheatley, *Leadership and the New Science* (San Francisco: Berrett-Koehler, 2006), pp. 34, 33.
[8]Ibid., p. 89.
[9]Ibid., p. 139
[10]If Wheatley were to embrace the truth that we were created in the image of the triune God, whose very nature is interdependence and interconnectedness, combined with Colossians 1:17, which tells us that "in him all things hold together," she would see the larger picture of human relationships in all its created complexity and beauty.
[11]Robert K. Greenleaf, *Servant Leadership* (New York: Paulist Press, 1977), p. 13.
[12]Ibid., p. 46.
[13]Burns, *Transforming Leadership*, p. 227.
[14]Ibid., p. 19.
[15]Ibid., p. 215.
[16]Ibid., p. 219.

[17]Margaret Wheatley, *Finding Our Way* (San Francisco: Berrett-Koehler, 2007), p. 18.

[18]Ibid., p. 46.

[19]Ibid., p. 46.

[20]Ibid., p. 52.

[21]Ibid., p. 53.

[22]Ibid., p. 57.

[23]Ibid., p. 130.

[24]Greenleaf, *Servant Leadership*, p. 13.

[25]Ibid., p. 14.

[26]Ibid., p. 46.

[27]This idea of using Jesus' life as a moral example for right living is similar to the late nineteenth-century "quest for the historical Jesus," in which it was believed that if we could strip away the supernatural mythology from the scriptural depiction of the life of Jesus, we would have a model of right behavior we could emulate. This quest emerged from the Moral Atonement theory of Adolf von Harnack and others, who jettisoned all supernatural claims of Scripture in order to find a core moral motif that they believed was the essence of the biblical story. Every attempt at focusing on Jesus' life as an example starts us on a dangerous road back in that direction.

[28]This is not meant as a direct critique of Ken Blanchard's book *Lead Like Jesus*, although I do not agree with his premise that "Jesus was the greatest leadership role model of all time." Blanchard's book is full of helpful teaching regarding the need for personal transformation in the heart of the leader and the call to servanthood as leaders. I wish only that he would have titled his book *Lead Because of Jesus*.

[29]Steve Korch, *My Soul Thirsts* (Valley Forge, Penn.: Judson Press, 2000), p. 32.

Chapter 4: Stewards of Our Relationship with Our Creator God

[1]This list was taken from Richard Foster, *The Celebration of Discipline* (San Francisco: Harper & Row, 1978).

[2] Ibid., p. 17.

[3]C. S. Lewis, *The Lion, the Witch and the Wardrobe* (New York: HarperCollins, 2001), p. 146.

[4]Douglas Webster, *Discipline of Surrender* (Downers Grove, Ill.: InterVarsity Press, 2001), p. 13.

[5]Hannah Whitehall Smith, *The Christian's Secret of a Happy Life* (Grand Rapids: Baker, 1952), pp. 27-28, 43.

[6]Oswald Chambers, *Enjoying Intimacy with God* (Chicago: Moody Press, 1980), pp. 13-14.

[7]Steve Korch, *My Soul Thirsts* (Valley Forge, Penn.: Judson Press, 2000), pp. 44-46.

[8]Ibid., p. 39.

[9]Ibid., p. 30.

[10]Excellent Cultures (www.excellentcultures.com) helps organizations understand and improve their culture. The first step in their Four-Step Data Driven Process to transform cultures measures the current reality of organizations and benchmarks

them against high-performance organizations. Their message is to focus not on where your culture is but on where it could improve and how performance would correspondingly improve.

[11]William Robinson, *Incarnate Leadership* (Grand Rapids: Zondervan, 2009), p. 84.

[12]Ibid., p. 86.

[13]Margaret Wheatley, *Leadership and the New Science* (San Francisco: Berrett-Koehler, 2006), p. 127.

[14]Ibid., p. 128.

[15]Ibid., p. 129 (italics added).

Chapter 5: Stewards of Our Relationship with Ourselves

[1]R. Scott Rodin, *The Four Gifts of the King* (Spokane: Kingdom Life, 2008).

[2]William Robinson, *Incarnate Leadership* (Grand Rapids: Zondervan, 2009), pp. 77-78.

[3]Michael Jinkins, *The Character of Leadership* (San Francisco: Jossey-Bass, 1998), p. 102.

[4]An example of this misplaced confidence is found in Bill George's popular leadership book, *True North* (San Francisco: Jossey-Bass, 2007), where he writes, "The key to self-acceptance is to love your self unconditionally. It's easy to love our strength and bask in our successes. To love ourselves unconditionally, we have to learn to accept ourselves as we are. Once armed with a high level of self-awareness and self-acceptance, it is much easier to regulate yourself and your feelings. Your anger and emotional outbursts usually result when someone penetrates to the core what you do not like about yourself, or still cannot accept. By accepting yourself just as you are, you are no longer vulnerable to those hurts, and are prepared to interact authentically with others who come into your life. Free of having to pretend to be something you're not, you can focus on pursuing your passions and fulfilling your dreams" (p. 82). At first blush this may look like an affirmation of my own formulation of the steward leader. But we need to ask about this "self-acceptance" and the admonition to "love yourself as you are." If self-acceptance is detached from the ongoing transformation of the Holy Spirit, conforming us to the image of Christ, then it is actually self-deception. When the enemy succeeds in getting us to "love ourselves as we are" instead of loving ourselves as bearers of the image of God, he has succeeded indeed.

[5]Max De Pree, *Leadership Is an Art* (New York: Broadway Business, 2004), p. 32.

[6]Arbinger Institute, *Leadership and Self-Deception* (San Francisco: Berrett-Koehler, 2002), p. 154. While this work by the Arbinger Institute is a helpful way of understanding these human relationships and the self-betraying behavior of leaders, it lacks the power to transform leaders that they may be truly "out of the box" toward others, or toward themselves. Without the transforming power of the Holy Spirit, this good teaching ends up throwing us back on ourselves to find ways to get out of our boxes, and that leads only to futility.

Chapter 6: Stewards of Our Relationship with Our Neighbor

[1]Margaret Wheatley, *Leadership and the New Science* (San Francisco: Berrett-Koehler, 2006), p. 87.

[2]Ibid., p. 89.

[3]Ibid., p. 165.

[4]Michael Jinkins, *The Character of Leadership* (San Francisco: Jossey-Bass, 1998), p. 93.

[5]Ibid., p. 119.

[6]Ibid., p. 5.

Chapter 7: Stewards of Our Relationship with God's Creation

[1]*Pantheism* is derived from the Greek words *pan* (all) and *theos* (God). It affirms that all reality is a unity and that unity is divine. Therefore, all reality is divine. According to this metaphysic, creation is inherently divine, which is our motivation for preserving it at all costs. By not recognizing the divinity of God in distinction to the goodness with which he endowed his creation, pantheists have made all things equal in divinity and end up worshipping creation.

[2]"Panentheism is a view that the universe is God, but God is more than the universe. For the panentheist, God has an identity of his own, that is, he is something that the universe is not. On the other hand, the universe is part of the reality of God. It is God." (Sinclair Ferguson, David F. Wright and J. I. Packer, *New Dictionary of Theology* [Downers Grove, Ill.: InterVarsity Press, 1988], p. 486.) Panentheists attempt to allow for uniqueness in the person of God and his divinity without creating a distinction between that divinity and the creation. While it has created a new category for the conversation, it remains problematic and unacceptable to a Christian cosmology. We worship only the Creator. He alone is divine and worthy of adoration. Our care for creation is not motivated by some inherent divinity, but solely because of the goodness with which God created it and because of his command for us to nurture and care for it.

[3]I give credit to Restoring Eden for this comment.

[4]*Webster's New Dictionary*, 2006, s.v. "nurture."

[5]Reprinted with permission from R. Scott Rodin, *The Seven Deadly Sins of Christian Fundraising* (Spokane: Kingdom Life, 2007).

[6]Richard Kriegbaum, *Leadership Prayers* (Wheaton, Ill.: Tyndale House, 1998), pp. 6-7.

BIBLIOGRAPHY

Arbinger Institute. *Leadership and Self-Deception.* San Francisco: Berrett-Koehler, 2002.

Barth, Karl. *Church Dogmatics,* trans. G. W. Bromiley and T. F. Torrance. Edinburgh: T&T Clark, 1956.

Bass, Bernard M. *Bass and Stogdill's Handbook of Leadership.* New York: Free Press, 1991.

Bonhoeffer, Dietrich. *The Cost of Discipleship.* New York: Macmillan, 1948.

Burns, James MacGregor. *Transforming Leadership.* New York: Grove Press, 2003.

Chambers, Oswald. *Enjoying Intimacy with God.* Chicago: Moody Press, 1980.

De Pree, Max. *Leadership Is an Art.* New York: Broadway Business, 2004.

Foster, Richard. *The Celebration of Discipline.* San Francisco: Harper and Row, 1978.

Greenleaf, Robert K. *The Servant as Leader.* Westfield, Ind.: Greenleaf Center, 1970.

—————. *Servant Leadership.* New York: Paulist Press, 1977.

Jinkins, Michael. *The Character of Leadership.* San Francisco: Jossey-Bass, 1998.

Korch, Steve. *My Soul Thirsts.* Valley Forge, Penn.: Judson Press, 2000.

Kriegbaum, Richard. *Leadership Prayers.* Wheaton, Ill.: Tyndale House, 1998.

Lewis, C. S. *The Lion, the Witch and the Wardrobe.* New York: HarperCollins, 2001.

McCullough, David. *John Adams.* New York: Simon and Schuster, 2001.

Nouwen, Henri. *In the Name of Jesus.* New York: Crossroads, 1996.

O'Toole, James. *Leading Change.* New York: Ballantine, 1995.

Robinson, Tri. *Small Footprint, Big Handprint.* Boise: Ampelon, 2008.

Robinson, William. *Incarnate Leadership.* Grand Rapids: Zondervan, 2009.

———. *Leading People from the Middle.* Provo, Utah: Executive Excellence, 2002.

Rodin, R. Scott. *The Four Gifts of the King.* Spokane: Kingdom Life, 2008.

Smith, Hannah Whitehall. *The Christian's Secret of a Happy Life.* Grand Rapids: Baker, 1952.

Webster, Douglas. *Discipline of Surrender.* Downers Grove, Ill.: InterVarsity Press, 2001.

Wheatley, Margaret. *Finding Our Way.* San Francisco: Berrett-Koehler, 2007.

———. *Leadership and the New Science.* San Francisco: Berrett-Koehler, 2006.

INDEX

The **Not-for-Profit** Practice of OneAccord))

OneAccord NFP helps transform not-for-profit organizations through professional partnership. We are a team of proven professionals who combine our skills and experience to provide you with the best available services to grow your not-for-profit organization. Our twofold commitment is to speak absolute truth with absolute compassion. Our mission is to help not-for-profit organizations, ministries and churches increase revenue, improve effectiveness and make successful transitions in leadership to fulfill their mission and realize their vision.

R. Scott Rodin is managing principal of OneAccord and also serves as senior fellow of the Engstrom Institute and on the boards of the Evangelical Environmental Network and ChinaSource. He may be contacted at:

R. Scott Rodin
Managing Principal, OneAccord
Not-for-Profit Practice
21816 N. Buckeye Lake Lane
Colbert, WA 99005
509-998-8553
scott.rodin@oneaccordpartners.com
www.oneaccordpartners.com/NFP